Turkish Coast

Front cover: Ölüdeniz lagoon

Right: Temple of Trajan, Pergamon

TOP 10 ATTRACTIONS

Antalya A beautiful and sophisticated city with a host of attractions *(page 70)*

Kaunos tombs, Dalyan A fine example of the Lycian tombs that are such a feature of this part of the Turkish Coast *(page 54)*

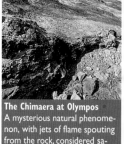

The Chimaera at Olympos A mysterious natural phenomenon, with jets of flame spouting from the rock, considered sacred in ancient times *(page 68)*

Pergamon • One of the greatest of the Graeco-Roman city states, home to one of the first health spas in history *(page 31)*

Bodrum Castle The massive Crusader Castle that looms over this little white town is now filled with fascinating marine treasures *(page 50)*

Gallipoli The peninsula where tens of thousands of Allied forces died and Atatürk made his reputation in World War I *(page 25)*

Ephesus Home to one of the seven wonders of the ancient world and now one of the world's best preserved ancient cities *(page 41)*

Ölüdeniz Famous for its shades of turquoise and blue lagoon, this is one of the Mediterranean's finest beaches *(page 57)*

Aspendos A superbly preserved ancient theatre, venue for an annual opera and ballet festival each summer *(page 76)*

Pamukkale A glorious cascade of travertine and limestone pools that shimmer, ever-changing with the light *(page 46)*

CONTENTS

82

29

12

Features

INTRODUCTION

Statistics might be able to tell you that Turkey grows 70 percent of the world's hazelnuts, but they don't even begin to describe the extraordinary physical beauty of the soaring cliffs and deep clear turquoise seas, the fresh scent of the umbrella pines in the heat of the summer sun, the shimmer of the full moon above the pools of Pamukkale, the simple joy of eating calamari on a shady terrace beside a traditional fishing harbour, and the mind-blowing history everywhere you look. Nevertheless, Turkey's vital statistics are fairly mind-bogglingly huge.

Geography and Landscape

The Turkish coast (not all of it covered in this book) is a staggering 7,200km (4,474 miles) in length, stretching along the shores of the Black Sea, the Bosphorus Straits (in Istanbul), the Sea of Marmara, the Dardanelles, the Aegean Sea (in the West) and the Mediterranean (in the South). Turkey connects Europe with Asia – in fact, only a tiny portion of the country is in Europe – a bridging function that has for centuries been an important element in the history of Asia Minor.

The west coast as far as Marmaris is characterised by bays, peninsulas reaching out into the Aegean and a hinterland dominated by

Left: dropping anchor on the Lycian coast

Population pattern

Two-thirds of Turkey's population live within about 30km (18 miles) of the coast, in one of the four giant cities – Istanbul, İzmir, Antalya and Adana or the many towns and ribbon developments that line the roads between them. Only the capital Ankara is out on a limb inland.

broad, fertile river valleys and alluvial plains. The best scenery is to be found a little further east, along the Lycian Coast between Fethiye and Antalya, where the Taurus Mountains swoop directly down to the sea. This region, which was called Lycia in antiquity, is a relatively difficult region to explore, although the construction of a coast road in the 1980s has helped to open it up. The scenery of the Bozburun Pensinsula, south of Marmaris, is also glorious. Here mountains over 2,000m (6,560ft) high soar directly from the seabed, their feet clad in sandy coves and caves carved by the crashing surf, their razor-sharp crowns encircled by the flight of mountain eagles. Between them, the pine forests and herbal scrub are a riot of colour and aroma in spring, while those lowland valleys not clad in a sea of plastic hothouses burst into blossom as the apples, oranges and almonds flower and then fruit. There are also some

Kaputaş cove on the Lycian Coast

very pretty areas along the north Aegean coast, while the south Aegean is generally flatter and more built-up.

The area immediately to the east of Antalya, sometimes described as the 'Turkish Riviera', has a broad fertile coastal plain – formerly known as Pamphilia – that makes for glorious long sandy beaches but rather boring views, and you have to go about 30km (18 miles) inland if you want mountains.

The ruins of ancient Knidos, near Marmaris

Historic Crossroads

Think of a great civilisation and chances are they will have had a foothold in Anatolia at some point– the Hittites, Persians, Greeks, Romans, Arabs, Turks and Ottomans, for starters. Cleopatra owned a small chunk, given to her as a wedding present by Mark Anthony. Norman crusaders set up kingdoms in Constantinople, Antioch and Edessa. Genghis Khan and his Mongol hordes swept through, briefly and violently. All of them left a physical legacy that has made this a breathlessly magnificent smorgasbord of history that spans several thousand years, many major cultures, several religions and figures such as Helen of Troy, Croesus (as in rich as...) and even Santa Claus (St Nicholas).

The Seljuk Turks after whom Atatürk chose to name his nation were in fact a small group who only arrived in Anatolia in the 12th century AD from their Central Asian homeland. Today, while the Turks are remarkably united

Studying marine life in
Marmaris

as a nation, this hotchpotch of history has created an extraordinary racial mix. The differences in features can be seen, from aquiline noses straight off a Grecian urn in the northwest, to the almost Mongol faces in the east and the sharp Arab features in the far south. About 20 percent of the country's population are Kurds; about 1 percent are Arab; 99 percent are Muslim.

East Meets West

Throughout its long history, Turkey has looked in two directions at once, acting as a trading route (part of the Silk Road), crossroads and political conduit between the great civilisations of Europe and the East. These days, Turkey is again pulled in two directions, between Atatürk's pro-Western, secular approach – those who want nothing more than to join the EU – and those who are looking East to Islam and traditional values. Battle is waging through the lawcourts and parliament and women, whether they choose to wear headscarves for religious reasons, as a fashion statement, for political motives or to keep the dust off their hair, are in the front line.

Most of the country is still strongly agricultural, a peasant land of women in baggy trousers and cardigans, men in flat caps, herds of goats and acres of plastic hothouses nursing the world's finest tomatoes and aubergines. But the major cities and resorts, most of them in a wafer-thin fringe around the coast, have a veneer of sophistication that matches any in the world, with fine dining and clubs filled with beautiful people in designer clothes and plenty of bling. Alongside them are increasing battalions of identikit villas and apartment blocks as the northern Europe dream of a place in the sun has reached the Turkish shore and started a Costas-style building stampede along the coast. Luckily, with so much coast, there's still plenty that is beautiful and unspoilt as well.

Choosing Your Spot

Which bit of coast is best for you? There is a rough division by nationality *(see below)*, but much more important is to choose by interest. There is ancient history absolutely everywhere you look, but if you want to explore the region in detail, either do a touring holiday or choose to stay in the Ayvalik area for visiting Pergamon, Gallipoli and Troy; Kuşadası for Ephesus, Aphrodisias, Didyma, Priene and

The National Divide

People have joked for years about the great Anglo-German sun-lounger battle, but in Turkey they took it one stage further, dividing up the coast. The Brits took the Aegaean and Turquoise Coast as far as Ölüdeniz and the Germans the stretch from Antalya to Alanya. Beyond Alanya was the province of the Turks and Arabs. The Lycian Coast between was a sort of gentrified no-man's land, shared by older, wealthier tourists of both nations. These days, it's getting more confused as British house-buyers head for the south coast, the Russians arrive en masse and the Turkish middle classes begin to head south for seaside holidays. With advertising now stretching as far as Beijing, expect Chinese signs to join the Cyrillic in the streets before too long.

Miletus; the Lycian Coast for an embarrassment of riches including Xanthos, the Letoön, Olympos and Phaselis; and Antalya or Belek for Perge and Aspendos.

Socially, Bodrum and Antalya are the most upmarket resorts, with more sedate Kaş and Kalkan close behind. Kuşadası and Ölüdeniz are at the lower end of the spectrum, although there are exceptions to all. Olympos, near Antalya, is the closest the coast has to a backpacker hangout, while Behramkale on the Aegean Coast is the favourite of Istanbul's artists and intellectuals. Belek is full of fanatical golfers. However, the truth is that little of this matters – most tourists either stay within the confines of their hotel or simply head down to the nearest beach.

İzmir woman in local dress

If you crave a long sandy beach, head for Patara or the area between Antalya and Alanya, which also has the shallowest sloping coast, making beaches great for small children. The Lycian Coast, west of Antalya, has fabulous scenery and great swimming, but few actual beaches (and many of them are pebbly and extremely steep), but is great for watersports, while the Turquoise Coast, around Bodrum and Marmaris, is perfect for watersports of all kinds from yachting and windsurfing to diving. The Aegean Coast is gentler and generally more family friendly.

A BRIEF HISTORY

Modern Turkey has had many identities across the millennia; some even claim this was the home of the garden of Eden. The earliest humanoid bones found date back some 1 million years. But the real human history of the region starts in around 9000BC, at the time when the first hunter-gatherers were beginning to worship at temples and the first farmers were growing grain (both near Urfa in southeast Turkey). By 7000BC, tent-dwellers were painting caves at Beldibi near Antalya and by 6400BC a community of around 5,000 were using irrigation, keeping domesticated sheep and pigs at Çatal Höyük, south of Konya, officially the second-oldest town in the world (after Jericho).

The Time of Legends

Fast forward to around 2000BC when the Hittites arrived further east, creating an empire in central Anatolia that lasted for 700 years and challenged the might of Babylon and Egypt. Meanwhile, on the Aegean coast, Troy had already been flourishing for around 1,000 years and was to continue happily trading and scrapping with its neighbours for almost another 800 years before the epic siege, in c.1250BC, that was immortalised by Homer in *The Iliad*. Most more prosaic commentators tend to agree that the war was probably more about trade routes than love but whatever the

The Trojan Horse

cause, the Trojan wars united the Greeks against a common enemy and the fallout created a diaspora that rewrote the map of Anatolia.

Greek diaspora

From the 12th century BC onwards, wave after wave of the so-called Sea People moved into and across Anatolia, the Hittite empire crumbling before them. First the Phrygians from Thrace and the northwest moved into the centre of the country, best-known for King Midas (of the golden touch; 7th century BC). Then the Lydians settled on the Aegean coast, with their capital at Sardis, again famed for a stupendously rich monarch, King Croesus (561–546BC), credited with the invention of both coins and dice. To the south, the wild Taurus mountains were settled by the Lycians, the greatest of the

Lycian Tombs

Proud inventors of the world's earliest known democratic federation (supposedly one of the models on which the constitution of the United States was based), the Lycians left surprisingly little in the way of archaeological evidence other than a large supply of extraordinarily elaborate tombs – 1,085 found at the last count. They come in many shapes and sizes. The earliest include the square-cut pillar tombs such as the Harpy Tomb at Xanthos, and there are also chunky free-standing sarcophagi with three compartments (for slaves and companions, for grave goods and for the main inhabitant) and an elaborate often Gothic lid like the keel of an upturned ship. More common are the rock-cut tombs cut into the cliff face, many modelled on private houses, even copying wooden carpenters' pegs in stone, the most elaborate, in Pinara and Myra mimicking grand temples. The dead lay on stone benches surrounded by grave goods, the entrance blocked by sliding doors and the whole edifice was carved and painted.

Lycian 'ship's keel' tombs on Kekova Island

early Hellenistic peoples, originally from Crete whom the Hittites described as a proudly independent, ungovernable, matriarchal society. The gentler lands east of modern Antalya were settled by the Pamphilians, and the eastern Mediterranean by the Cilicians. Inland, from 800BC, there was a second flowering of a smaller neo-Hittite kingdom.

Clash of the Titans

All these people were builders and traders, creating great cities along the coast, such as Ephesus, a great port and cult centre sacred to Artemis, which traded not only with each other and with Europe, but with the caravans from the east. It was a conspicuous display of wealth that inevitably drew envious eyes.

In 546BC, Cyrus II of Persia invaded, turning the region into a nominal colony for nearly 200 years until, in 334BC, Alexander of Macedonia (the Great) turned his greedy young eyes on Anatolia, conquering King Darius of Persia at the epic battle of Issos in 333BC.

Anatolia became Greek again, but Alexander was better at conquering than ruling and he continued east, only to die, absurdly young, in 323BC. Anatolia was divided between four of his generals – Seleukos Nicator, Ptolemy, Antigonus and Lysimachus. With the influence of classical Greece at its height, the sale of marble went through the roof as temples and colonnades, baths, theatres and all the other essentials of sophisticated city life were erected and decorated with magnificent statuary. Monuments that survive today, from the great theatre at Aspendos to the temple at Didyma and the great marble-paved streets and forum of Perge, rose in glory. The city states flourished, gradually gaining their independence then linking together in political federations such as the powerful Lycean League, first established by Pericles in the 4th century BC.

The Temple of Athena at Priene

Romans and Christians

Then, in 133BC, the king of Pergamon bequeathed his kingdom to Rome. Within a few years, Anatolia had become the Roman province of Asia Minor. The city states lost their independence but gained the powerful protection of the *pax romana*. Fresh invasion attempts by the Goths and Persians were repulsed and Mediterranean piracy was cleaned up by Pompey. Mark Anthony met Cleopatra in Tarsus and married her near Antioch (mod-

St Nicholas (Baba Noël), who attended the Council of Nicaea

ern Antakya), which is also where Sts Peter, Paul and Barnabas supposedly met in a hidden cave church and decided on a name for the new religion – Christianity.

In AD40 St Paul began preaching Christianity across Anatolia but the authorities soon clamped down. Peter and Barnabas were only two of many martyrs, but the religion continued to spread, with the caves of Cappadocia, for example, riddled with cave churches. It was 313 before Emperor Constantine stopped persecuting the Christians, eventually making it the state religion and sending his mother (St Helena) to Jerusalem on a relic hunt. In 325, he called the Council of Nicaea (İznik) which settled the basic tenets of faith in the Nicene Creed.

The Byzantine Empire

Although he grew up in Diocletian's court, Constantine was always more at home further east. In 330, with Rome under severe pressure from the barbarians, he chose the site of his new capital with the help of an angel and Constantinople grew from the small Greek city of Byzantium. Shortly after his death, the Roman Empire split in two and the glory that became the Byzantine Empire was born. It was an era of orthodox Christianity, extreme wealth and opulence, fed as ever by international trade with both east and west, and of extreme courtly intrigue. With power centralised in the north, the importance of the coastal cities began to decline, their wealth declining further as many of their harbours silted up, pushing them inland and away from the coast.

Islam and the Iconoclasts

Yet still the opulence of the Byzantine Empire drew the vultures – the Slavs from the west, the Avars from the east and the Sassanid Persians from the southeast. But in 654 came a new and very different threat as Muhammed's newly converted Arab warriors powered their way to the very gates of Constantinople and were only finally defeated after a 20-year siege. A second invasion in 717–18 brought much of the empire under Islamic rule for the first time.

Christianity was tolerated, but Christians were paid less and charged more tax, so many chose to convert. Others adopted the iconoclastic beliefs of Islam, gouging out the faces on frescoes, mosaics and sculptures. In 863, Byzantium began to fight back and eventually, by 1014, recovered all its possessions. But by that time, Islam was here to stay.

The Seljuks

In 1071 came a new threat from the Asian steppes, the Turkoman Seljuks who routed the Byzantine Army and captured the emperor at the Battle of Manzikert, swallowing up half their empire and setting up their own empire, the Sultanate of Rum, based in Konya. This crucially took control of several key Mediterranean ports, including Alanya and

Antalya, and much of the Silk Road, along which they built a series of caravanserais (inns), bridges and roads that offered five-star facilities to travellers who could cross their lands in safety and comfort. Their rule was in many ways a golden age, but it proved very short-lived, utterly destroyed by the Mongol invasions of Genghis Khan in 1243.

The Crusades

Meanwhile, poor Byzantium was in trouble all round. Subject Armenia chose its moment of weakness to try and break away. The Mongols were not satisfied with destroying the Seljuks and in the west, the sight of Muslims controlling the Holy Lands was too much for Catholics to bear. Crusader armies gathered and began tramping across Byzantine lands, docking in Byzantine ports and helping themselves to anything they wanted along the way. As the Normans won lands that had once been Byzantine, they held onto them and set up their own kingdoms in Jerusalem, Antioch (modern Antakya) and Edessa (modern Sanliurfa). By 1203, the Fourth Crusade, fed up with the idea of going as far as Jerusalem, stopped halfway and sacked Constantinople itself; the emperors fled to Nicaea and only got their city back in 1261.

Crusaders sack Constantinople

Piri Reis

Piri Reis (full name Hadji Muhiddin Piri Ibn Hadji Mehmed; c.1465–1555) was an Ottoman admiral, explorer and cartographer – Nelson, Columbus and Ptolemy rolled into one – best known for his magnificent world maps (1513 and 1528). There is a small museum dedicated to him in his home town of Gelibolu (see page 27).

The Ottoman Empire

As the Seljuks battled against the Mongols, a small bunch of warriors led by Ertuğrul Ghazi and his son Osman, first helped them, then took over their lands, creating a new Ottoman Empire with its capital, from 1326, in Bursa. All the Aegean and Mediterranean coasts came under Ottoman rule and here they remained until the end of World War I.

In 1453, Sultan Mehmet II eventually conquered Constantinople, and changed its name to Istanbul. The Ottoman Empire expanded rapidly and arrived at its golden age during the lengthy reign of Süleyman the Magnificent (1520–66), who not only doubled the size of the empire, but was known as 'the Lawgiver' and who, together with his great architect, Sinan, left Turkey a legacy of many of its finest buildings, notably its distinctive mosques.

Unfortunately many of his successors were not as wise and the severe competition for the throne meant that many of the best never made it to adulthood alive or sane. Over the centuries the great empire slowly crumbled, held together by a slave army of janissaries, Jewish and Genoese and Western European bankers and businessmen. The janissaries eventually got out of control and in 1825, Sultan Mahmut II lost patience and had around 5,000 of them massacred; the bankers had their own agenda; and Greece, Egypt, Lebanon and other territories succeeded in declaring independence. By 1854, the empire was only saved from Russia during the Crimean War by French and British intervention.

World War I and Atatürk's Republic

From the 1870s onwards, pressure began to build for more democratic rule, led by a group who became known as the Young Turks. Among their number was a fiery young military commander, Mustafa Kemal. At the outbreak of World War I, the Ottomans chose to ally themselves with the Germans. A massive and disastrous Allied invasion at Gallipoli followed in 1915. The defence was led by Kemal, who became a national hero. In 1919, the Treaty of Sèvres carved up Ottoman lands with all the Allies claiming some territory.

It was too much for Kemal, who used his new-found stature to lead a bloodless coup that toppled the Sultan and the Ottoman Empire. He then drew up the borders of modern Turkey (ignoring Kurdish and Armenian claims) and, in the ensuing War of Independence, chased out the foreigners, ending with a vicious battle on the docks of İzmir against the Greeks. In 1923 an estimated 1.5 million Greeks and Turks moved house in an official exchange of populations.

Kemal took the name Atatürk (Father Turk), became president of the new Turkish Republic, and set about transforming society, abolishing polygamy, legalising alcohol, outlawing the fez and the turban, dervish orders and other religious brotherhoods, making edu-

Kemal Atatürk

cation for women compulsory, introducing the Latin script and Georgian calendar and a secular constitution that enshrined equality for all.

Modern History

Since then Turkey has carefully trodden the divide between East and West, run as a multi-party democracy, but with the military always waiting in the wings to ensure that government remains true to Atatürk's ideals. Bizarrely, there have been four military coups, with the military stabilising the country and returning it to the 'correct' democratic track. Turkey was a founder member of the UN and is a member of NATO, but is criticised for its human rights record, particularly in relation to the difficult Kurdish question. PKK Kurdish separatists have been waging a terrorist war since the 1970s that resulted in thousands of deaths on both sides and currently has Turkish troops running regular incursions into northern Iraq.

In 1974, Turkey invaded northern Cyprus in support of its citizens on the island, producing huge tensions with Greece that continue to block its attempts to join the EU. The country has also been hit by al-Qaeda terrorist attacks, bird flu and earthquakes. But every attempt to knock this fabulous country flat fails. The economy is booming, winter turns the coast into one giant construction site, it is rapidly overtaking Spain as Europe's favourite holiday destination – the heartland of great empires is striking back.

A face of modern Turkey

Historical Landmarks

3rd millennium BC Regional principalities such as Troy in the Aegean are founded.

c.1250–650BC The Trojan Wars are followed by the Greek diaspora.

546BC Persian King Cyrus the Great conquers Anatolia.

334–323BC The campaigns of Alexander the Great.

4th–2nd centuriesBC Era of the Hellenistic city states.

133BC King Attalus III of Pergamon leaves his kingdom to Rome; Anatolia eventually becomes the Roman province of Asia Minor.

AD325 The Council of Nicaea proclaims Christianity the official religion of the Roman Empire.

330 Constantine moves his capital to Byzantium (Constantinople).

647 Arab invasions mark the introduction of Islam to Anatolia.

1071 Selçuk Turks rout the Byzantine army at the Battle of Malazgirt.

1096–1204 Crusaders use Anatolian ports; Edessa and Antioch briefly become Norman principalities.

1243 The Selçuks are defeated by the Mongols.

1288 Muslim warlord, Osman Ghazi, begins to build a power base.

1453 Ottoman Sultan Mehmet II conquers Constantinople

1512–20 Selim I consolidates Ottoman rule over Anatolia, and assumes the title of Caliph, head of all Islam.

1520–66 Reign of Süleyman the Magnificent.

1908 Young Turks Revolution in support of Western-style liberalism.

1914–18 Turkey enters World War I as a German ally; Mustafa Kemal leads victorious resistance at Gallipoli.

1923 Mustafa Kemal (now called Atatürk) abolishes the monarchy and becomes president of the new republic of Turkey. War of Independence and exchange of populations with Greece.

1946 Turkey becomes a charter member of the UN.

1952 Turkey joins NATO.

1974 Turkey invades northern Cyprus.

1980s PKK launches guerilla warfare against Turkish Government.

2005 Negotiations on Turkey joining the EU begin.

WHERE TO GO

The Turkish Coast stretches all the way from the Dardanelles to Antakya near the Syrian border. This section focuses on the areas most popular with western tourists, covering the Aegean and the Mediterranean as far east as Alanya. It is divided into chapters and takes in all the main resorts as well as excursions to ancient sites.

THE NORTH AEGEAN

Known today as the Dardanelles, but to the ancients as the Hellespont, a narrow strait, only 1,200m (3,937ft) at its narrowest point, marks the division of Europe and Asia at the northern point of the Aegean coast. It has proved a strategic and romantic challenge to both military heroes and brave fools. Leander swam across by night to visit his lover, Hero; English poet Lord Byron swam across for fun in 1810. The Persian army, led by Xerxes, crossed the strait on a bridge of boats in 480BC in a failed bid to conquer Greece; Alexander crossed it in 334BC to defeat the Persians. On its north shore is the Gallipoli Peninsula; just to the south is Troy. This is truly a fitting introduction to a coast of legends.

Gallipoli (Gelibolu)

Those who are not military historians might shy away from visiting **Gallipoli**, but no one who comes here could fail to be moved by the immense tragedy and dignity of the story told across this beautiful and now peaceful peninsula. On 25 April 1915, at the instigation of an inexperienced Winston Churchill, in his first major role as First Lord of the

Left: Kaş on the Lycian Coast

Admiralty, the Allies launched an ill-conceived attack on the Dardanelles in an attempt to gain control of the sea route through to the Black Sea. General von Sanders, the German commander of the Ottoman armies, handed over to his deputy, a brilliant and ruthless young Turkish officer, Mustafa Kemal (later Atatürk). 'I am not ordering you to attack, I am ordering you to die,' he proclaimed. And they did – in their thousands. Some 46,000 Allied troops and 86,000 Turkish troops were killed, and hundreds of thousands more were injured on both sides, before the Allies withdrew in defeat that Christmas. Many of the Allied casualties came from the Australian and New Zealand Army Corps (ANZAC), and Anzac Day (25th April) is still commemorated by both countries.

There are numerous guided tours of the peninsula from Çanakkale and even from Istanbul, or you can take the car ferry and explore the region on your own. Much of the scenic

Turkish War Memorial at Morto Bay

peninsula is now a national park, rich in plant and bird life. There are plaques at key sites and literature available at the two official museums and information points, the **Çamburnu Park Headquarters**, 1km (½ mile) south of Eceabat, and at the moving **Kabatepe Military Museum**, also the official Turkish memorial, at the centre of the peninsula. Both are open daily 8.30am–6pm; charge. Of the many well-tended cemeteries and other monuments to the dead that mark the former battlefields, the most famous are the **Lone Pine Cemetery** and **Anzac Cove**, where Australian and New Zealand troops are buried. The British landings were in the far south.

Also on the peninsula, 60km (40 miles) from most of the battlefields, is the historic port town of **Gelibolu** where the Ottoman tower is home to **Piri Reis Museum** museum (Tue–Sun 8.30am–noon, 1–5pm; free) dedicated to the great Ottoman cartographer *(see page 20).*

Side by side

"There is no difference between the Johnnies and the Mehmets to us,
Where they lie side by side here in this country of ours...
You, the mothers who sent their sons from far-away countries, wipe away your tears;
Your sons are now lying in our bosom and are in peace after having lost their lives on this land
They have become our sons as well."

Atatürk's poem to the fallen of Gallipoli

Çanakkale

Ferries cross frequently between Eceabat and **Çanakkale**, on the south shore of the Dardanelles, the largest town in the region, with a cluster of reasonable hotels, a pleasant promenade with great views across the straits and a couple of good seafood restaurants. It makes a good base for exploring the area. About 1km (½ mile) from the centre, the 15th-century **Ottoman fort** now contains a military museum (Tue–Wed, Fri–Sun 9am–noon, 1.30–5pm; fortress grounds daily 9am–10pm in summer; 9am–5pm in winter; charge) while the **Archaeology Museum** (1.5km/1 mile south of the centre on the Troy road; Tue–Sun 8.30am–noon, 1–5.30pm; charge) contains many of the finds from Troy.

Troy

For centuries, people thought Homer's stories of the siege of **Troy** and the voyages of Odysseus to be pure myth, but while the tall tales of gods and monsters can perhaps be taken with a pinch of salt, *The Iliad* and *The Odyssey* have some basis in fact. According to Homer, Paris, son of King Priam of Troy, kidnapped Helen, wife of King Menelaus of Sparta, the most beautiful woman in the world, and took her as his wife. Menelaus, his brother, King Agamemnon, and an army of Greeks including the great heroes Achilles, Hector and Odysseus, set sail with an armada of 1,000 ships, laying siege to Troy for many years. Eventually they came up with the idea of a wooden horse left as a gift outside the gate. The overly trusting Trojans wheeled it into the city, but that night, Greek soldiers crept from its belly and opened the gates and so the war was won and the phrase was born 'Beware of Greeks bearing gifts!'

It was 1873 before German archaeologist Heinrich Schliemann discovered the site that he claimed to be Troy (some authorities still dispute this), 32km (20 miles) south from

Çanakkale (daily 8am–7.30pm in summer; 8am–5pm in winter; charge). It is a complicated place to visit, with at least nine city layers covering some 6,000 years. Take a site map with you to make sense of it all. Schliemann's greatest find, a rich haul of treasure that he attributed to King Priam, was in fact nearly 1,000 years older. It vanished for a while, turning up recently in Russia's Pushkin Museum. Turkey's attempts to get back their loot have so far been unsuccessful.

Behramkale (Assos)

Popular amongst the arty set from Istanbul, **Behramkale**, on the Bay of Edremit, 70km (40 miles) south of Troy, is one of the prettiest villages on the Turkish coast. With no beach and little room for building, it has never developed mass-market tourism. Instead, a number of excellent small historic house hotels cluster round the little fishing port at the foot of the

Trojan columns

steep cliff. Some 240m (785ft) above the port, the ancient city of **Assos** (daily 8.30am–sunset; charge) has stupendous views across to the Greek island of Lesbos. Thought originally to have been a 13th-century BC Hittite settlement, it truly took root in the 8th century BC with the arrival of settlers from Lesbos. In 340BC, Aristotle founded a school of philosophy here; and St Paul preached here in later years; but the Byzantines largely destroyed the 6th-century BC Temple of Athena. What they left is currently being restored, along with a particularly fine necropolis (the town was famed for exporting sarcophagi) and about 3km (2 miles) of the old city walls, which stand up to a height of 14m (46ft) in places.

From Assos it's worth heading inland to the farming town of **Ayvacık**, renowned as a centre for weaving dobag carpets, and famed for its annual *panayır*, an entertaining week-long festival with ancient Greek origins, held in late April.

Behramkale

Ayvalık

At the southern end of the
Gulf of Edremit, 131km (81
miles) south of Behramkale.
Ayvalık (the 'place of the
quince') was a Greek city,
virtually abandoned during
the 1923 exchange of population. It has since been re-
populated and has grown
massively but the centre still
has a strongly Greek influence and immense charm,
with a town centre fishing
harbour overlooking a bay
scattered with islets, includ-

Ayvalık facade

ing **Cunda** (also known as Alibey Adası) where Ptolemy and
the Plinys liked to stay when they were in the area. Several
of the Greek Orthodox churches have been converted into
mosques. The beach resort for the town is actually several
kilometres south, at Sarımsaklı, which has little of the
charm, but does have good sand and watersports. The area
is a major producer of olive oil.

It is possible to do sightseeing trips from here across to
the Greek island of **Lesbos**.

Pergamon

Head south south of Ayvalık on Route E87 for 54km (33
miles) to **Pergamon,** once the most glamorous city in Asia
Minor. Although originally founded in the 8th century BC,
Pergamon was made over in golden glory in the 4th century
BC. Alexander the Great left much of his fortune here in the
care of his trusted general, Lysimachus, who, in turn, left it
with his trusted eunuch, Philetarus. After both Alexander

Part of the Temple of Trajan at Pergamon

and Lysimachus died, Philetarus refused to give back the 10,000 gold talents, using the money to build a complete new city instead. The subsequent line of rulers, known as the Attalids, went on to be hugely successful, and by 190BC Pergamon (also known as Pergamum) was in control of half of Asia Minor. In 133BC, King Attalus III changed the history of the world by willing his vast territories to Rome.

The city had all the usual trimmings, but also three truly outstanding features that made it famous throughout the ancient world. It was a religious centre of note, mixing worship of Zeus, the emperors and exotic Egyptian deities with that of the city's patron goddess, Athena, and the normal Greek pantheon; it became a place of healing *(see page 33)*; and it had a library fit to rival the Great Library at Alexandria. In fact, rivalry between the two was so intense that the Egyptians refused to let the Pergamene have papyrus and the scribes had to invent a new material of treated animal skin (parchment) on which to write. At its apogee, the library contained some 200,000 volumes, but in 41BC Mark Anthony gave most of it to Cleopatra as a gift, perhaps to replace the thousands of scrolls that went up in flames when Julius Caesar inadvertently set fire to Alexandria in 48BC.

There are two distinct areas of ruins – the **Acropolis** and the **Aesclepion**. They are about 8km (5 miles) apart, and a long, steep climb from the town centre; there is a taxi rank near the museum. Both sites are open daily 8.30am–5.30pm, until 7pm in summer (separate entrance charges). Allow plenty of time to explore here.

The Aesclepion was built in the 2nd century BC, with a temple, healing springs, theatre, medical school and accommodation *(see below)*. But the main body of the city is on the Acropolis, 300m (1,000ft) above the city with superb 360° views. At the highest point stand the partially restored Corinthian columns of the 3rd-century BC Temple of Trajan. Just below are the remains of the Temple of Athena, mentioned in the Biblical *Book of Revelations* as 'the place where Satan has his altar'. The altar in question, the fabulously carved Altar of Zeus, with a frieze depicting the battle between the gods and the giants, was taken to Germany in the 19th century and is now in Berlin's Pergamon Museum, along with much of the

Medicine at the Aesclepion

According to legend, Aesclepios, the son of Apollo, and the Greek god of Healing was a doctor in Agamemnon's army at Troy, who used the blood of the Gorgon to restore slain men to life. His emblem, a snake curled about a winged staff, is still the symbol of the medical profession. His temple and 'wellness' centre at Pergamon became one of the greatest healing centres in the ancient world under the masterful tutelage of Galen (c.129–99BC), considered to be the first great physician in Western history. Treatments included sleeping in the temple of Aesclepios, after which the priests would interpret your dreams, colonic irrigation and walking through a tunnel while the doctor whispered a cure in your ear, but Galen was also the first to discover that arteries carried blood. His treatments were still standard practices 1,500 years later.

other choice portable art from the site. The **theatre**, dramatically built into the hillside, could hold 10,000. It had a removable wooden stage and sound screen while the river below was dammed to create an artificial lake for naval battles involving galleons manned by hundreds of gladiators and slaves.

Below, in the town of **Bergama**, the **Kızıl Avlu** (Red Basilica; daily 8am–5pm, until 6.30pm in summer; charge) was founded in the 2nd century BC as a temple to the Egyptian god Serapis, and converted to a Christian basilica, listed in the *Book of Revelations* as one of the Seven Churches of the Apocalypse. The **Pergamon Arkeoloji Müsezi** (Archaeological Museum; Cumhuriyet Caddesi; Tue–Sun 8.30am–noon, 1–7pm, 5pm in winter; charge) houses those finds not taken to Berlin. Across the river, in the old Turkish quarter, Bergama has a great bazaar surrounding the **Ulucamii** (Grand Mosque), commissioned by Sultan Beyazıt I in 1398–99.

Foça

Much of the Aegean is rapidly getting built up. In the midst of all the construction, the Foça Peninsula is relatively undeveloped, with long stretches of well-protected coastline. **Eski Foça** (Old Foça), the site of ancient Phocaea, has a wonderful location, a Genoese fortress, and a number of restored Ottoman-Greek houses. The region is also home to one of the last colonies of the rare Mediterranean mark seal, although they are almost never seen. Nearby **Yeni Foça** (New Foça) has several good hotels and restaurants.

Foça local

Kuşadası from Pigeon Island

THE SOUTH AEGEAN

The South Aegean might be the most touristy area in the whole of Turkey but it is easy to see why, with its captivating mix of sandy beaches and turquoise seas, pine forests and amazing archaeological heritage – not to mention wonderful shops, restaurants and hotels.

İzmir

The third largest city in Turkey with a population of nearly 4 million, **İzmir**, once known as Smyrna, claims to be the birthplace of Homer (8th century BC) and there has been habitation here for over 7,000 years. But the city's confirmed history starts in the 4th century BC with Alexander the Great who built a fortified settlement. Set on a huge horseshoe bay, its superb harbour, a key outlet to the Mediterranean at the end of the Silk Road, has ensured that

İzmir has always prospered. Until World War I, it was a glamorous international city, but that changed during the last days of the bitter War of Independence as the Greek army and thousands of refugees converged on the docks amidst bitter fighting against Atatürk's forces. On 9 September 1922, the city went up in flames and more than 30,000 people died.

İzmir's former pizzazz has now been restored and the seafront promenade is lined with an opulent combination of palms, cafés and yachts. At its centre is a square, **Konak Meydanı**, with a pretty little mosque, the **Konak Camii** (1748), the **Saat Kulesi**, a decorative clock tower built in 1901 to help convert the Turks to western timekeeping,

İzmir's seafront clock tower

and a monument dedicated to the first Turkish soldier to lose his life during the Greek invasion of 1920. To the south, in Bahribaba Park, are the city's Archaeological and Ethnographic Museums (both open Tue–Sun 8.30am–5.30pm; charge). The **Arkeoloji Müzesi** has finds from nearby sites, including some fine classical statuary, while the **Etnografya Müzesi**, housed in a restored late-Ottoman hospital, has interesting photos and reconstructed buildings showing what the city was like pre-1922.

Walk through the back streets from here and you find yourself in the **Kemer-**

altı bazaar, one of the largest in Turkey, a gloriously eclectic mix of everything from leather jackets to live chickens. Behind this, at the foot of the castle, lies Alexander the Great's **Agora** (Namazgah; daily 8.30am–noon, 1–5pm; charge), rebuilt by Marcus Aurelius after an earthquake in AD178.

Shop in Kemeraltı bazaar

The best views of the city are from above. Climb (or take a taxi) up to the **Kadifekale** (Velvet Fortress), first built by Alexander but rebuilt and used by everyone since; its final ruined incarnation is a 500-year-old Ottoman fortress. To the north, you will see a huge open area, the **Kültür Parkı**, the city's main park but also home to restaurants, clubs, exhibitions and the **İzmir Tarih ve Sanat Müzesi** (History and Art Museum; Tue–Sun 8.30am–5.30pm; charge), a fascinating museum that includes a sumptuous collection of Hellenistic, Roman and Byzantine jewellery, along with statuary and ceramics from the 6th century BC to the Ottoman period. Just to the south of the park, the **Ahmet Piristina Museum of Metropolitan History and Archive** (Şair Eref Bulvarı 1a, Çankaya; daily 9am–6pm; free) is a converted fire station, charting the city's 7,000-year history (in Turkish and English), with special reference to its fires.

To round off the day, take the 19th-century **Asansör** (elevator; 7am–late), or climb the stairs beside it, up to the beautifully restored old Asansör district, once the Jewish quarter, where you can have a drink, a meal *(see page 137)* and watch the sun set over the city.

Çeşme harbour and castle

Çeşme Peninsula

Pushing west into the Aegean from İzmir, the **Çeşme Peninsula** is a holiday playground for wealthy Turks and, increasingly, for the international jetset, with a perfect blend of great beaches, marinas, and natural hot springs that have spawned some ravishingly good spas, all close to a major city with great shopping, an international airport and some very good restaurants.

Located some 80km (50 miles west of İzmir on Route 300, **Çeşme** (whose name means 'drinking fountain') is a pretty town with a 14th-century Genoese **Castle of St Peter** (daily 8.30am–5pm; charge) with displays of sculpture, coins and artefacts from nearby Ildırı (Erythrai) and a 16th-century caravanserai, built by Suleyman the Magnificent and now once again a hotel.

The resorts are spread along some 29km (18 miles) of the surrounding beaches, the most popular centres being **Dalyanköy** (5km/3 miles north of Çeşme); **Ilıca** (5km/3 miles east of Çeşme) which has thermal hot springs offering therapeutic treatments as well as pampering and several excellent spa hotels along with white-gold sands and turquoise seas; and **Alaçatı** (2km/1 mile beyond Ilıca), noted for its great windsurfing, trendy nightlife and mastic farms – the only place in Turkey where this highly prized aromatic resin is grown.

Sardis (Sart)

Detour inland for 90km (55 miles) to visit **Sardis** (Route 300, east of İzmir; daily 8am–noon, 1–5pm; charge), once the richest city in Asia Minor. The capital of the Lydian kings, it lay at the junction of the roads between Ephesus, Smyrna, Pergamon and the east, and the Lydians profited from every passing traveller. Not only that – the surrounding hills were rich in gold. In the 6th century BC, the last of the Lydians, King Croesus, invented coins and dice but got a little too flashy, giving away 10 tons of gold. At this point Persian eyes were drawn to his stash. Croesus consulted the Delphic Oracle who replied that if he attacked the Persian king, Cyrus the Great, a great empire would fall. Croesus went ahead, but unfortunately the wrong empire fell. Amongst the many ruins, highlights include the vast **Temple of Artemis**, begun in the 4th century

Blue Cruising

There can be few things more perfect than drifting gently along one of the world's most beautiful coasts in a traditional wooden gulet, stopping to swim or dive off where you choose, sunbathe in deserted coves, snorkel amidst the marble columns of a Byzantine city toppled by an earthquake into the sea. And all this can be yours on one of Turkey's famous blue cruises. Whether you choose to go for a day or several, join a tour or hire a whole boat for your own party – the options are limitless and the prices very affordable. Do your homework. A gulet traditionally sleeps between 6 and 14 people although they can be larger; comes with both sail and motor; and comes fully equipped and staffed. If you have your own boat, you can set your own itinerary, eat on board, have barbecues on the beach or moor up in town for a night on the tiles, as you prefer. Many tour operators offer this as an option (see pages 88–9) or you can wander along any harbour and see if you can do a deal locally, although this is obviously more fraught with difficulties.

Detail of mosaic flooring at
Sardis synagogue

BC but destroyed by an earthquake in AD17 before it was completed; the beautifully restored **Marble Court** of the 3rd-century AD gymnasium; and the impressive 3rd-century AD **synagogue**, the largest ancient synagogue outside of Palestine and a reminder of the sizeable and prosperous Jewish community that lived here during the city's Roman period.

Selçuk

For many centuries, Selçuk was nothing but a satellite village to the great port city of Ephesus, a few miles to the south, but in the 5th century AD, Ephesus harbour silted up and as the city died, Selçuk grew. These days it is a small provincial town with a few interesting sites. The **Selçuk Museum** (Ataturk Mahallesi, Kusadasi Caddesi; Tue–Sun 8.30am–noon, 12.30–5pm, till 7pm in summer; charge) is home to many of the finds from Ephesus and other nearby sites, including sumptuous statues of the 'many-breasted' Artemis and a playful bronze of Eros riding a dolphin.

On **Ayasoluk Hill**, above the town, is an ancient citadel. It was here, in about AD100, that St John the Evangelist, one of Christ's twelve apostles, supposedly died and was buried. In the 6th century AD, Emperor Justinian built a magnificent **basilica** around his tomb (daily 8am–5pm; charge). This was destroyed by the Mongols in the 15th century, but the setting is still both imposing and moving – an important Christian pilgrimage site. At the foot of the hill is the **İsa Bey Mosque** (daily 9am–6pm), built in 1365.

On the way out of town, heading towards Ephesus, pause briefly next to a scrubby field where a few bits of fallen marble are all that remain of the once glorious **Temple of Artemis** or **Diana** (daily 8.30am–5.30pm; charge), a temple so dazzling it was one of the seven wonders of the ancient world. First built in the 7th century BC, enlarged by Lydian King Croesus, rebuilt by Alexander and sacked by the Goths in AD263, it was eventually stripped down by Justinian, its stones reused in Istanbul's Aya Sofya and Selçuk's St John's Basilica.

Ephesus

In Roman times, **Ephesus** (3km/2 miles west of Selçuk; daily 8am–4.30pm, till 7pm in summer; charge) was the glistening jewel on the Aegean coast. A dazzling city founded by immigrants from Athens in about 1000BC, it thrived on the prof-

The 2nd-century BC Library of Celsus at Ephesus

its from its harbour under the Lydians, Persians, Greeks and Romans, only eventually dying when its harbour silted up in the 5th century AD; it now lies several kilometres inland. St Paul preached here, writing letters to the Ephesians that make up part of the New Testament.

The site is vast, extraordinarily well-preserved and well-restored. To do things the easy way, take a taxi from the main car park at the bottom to the Magnesian Gate at the top of the site and walk down. Walk along the colonnaded road, past private houses and shops to the Temple of Artemis. The Street of Kuretes heads downhill past the East Gymnasium, Upper Agora and Odeon, a 'studio' theatre for concerts and poetry. The small 2nd-century AD Temple of Hadrian is further down on the right, with the **Baths of Scholastica** behind it – look out for the communal toilets. and beautifully draped, headless statue of the bath's bene-factor. Opposite are a large mosaic and steps leading up to the late Roman and early Byzantine **terrace houses** (not always open) decorated with frescoes and mosaics.

On the corner with Marble Avenue, the city's **brothel** is signed by a footprint in the stone. Inside, rooms surround-ing the central atrium have decoration that suit the pur-pose while in the main re-ception area is a mosaic of the four seasons. Just off Marble Avenue, on the left, the superbly restored **Library of Celsus** was built in the 2nd century AD by the Roman Consul Gaius Julius Aquila and destroyed by Goths in AD 262. Between times, it housed some 12,000

Deliverance

During the worst of the persecutions, seven Chris-tians took refuge in a cave a few hundred metres east of the Ephesus and fell asleep. When they woke up and returned to town, they found that 200 years had passed, Christianity had be-come the state religion and they were safe.

scrolls. Its benefactor was buried in an ornate sarcophagus under the western wall.

Further on, the 24,000-seat **theatre** stands at one end of the **Arcadian Way**, the colonnaded main street down to the harbour. It was so sophisticated that by the 5th century AD, its covered walkways had street lamps at night (along with only Rome and Antioch). Other buildings to watch out for along here including the huge 2nd-century AD Harbour Baths and Gymnasium and the Church of the Virgin Mary, the the first in history dedicated to the Virgin.

The theatre, at the end of the Arcadian Way

Return to Marble Avenue and turn left to visit the 70,000-seat **stadium** and the 2nd-century Gymnasium of Vedius before leaving by the city's well-preserved monumental main gate.

An old legend claimed that the Virgin Mary came to Ephesus with St John and lived her last days here. In the early 19th century, a German nun, Catherine Emmerich, had a vision of her house and a century later, some Lazarist monks found a house that matched. In 1967, Pope Paul VI arrived and declared it authentic. Today, the **Meryemana** (Virgin Mary's House; Kusadasi Caddesi, 5km (3 miles) east of Ephesus; 7.30am–sunset) is a major pilgrimage site, with special services on 15 August and the first Sunday of October.

Kuşadası

About 20km (12 miles) southwest of Selçuk on Route 515, **Kuşadası** is probably the most popular resort on the Aegean coast, with a crowded marina as well as a busy cruise terminal, plenty of shops and restaurants, clubs and bars. The only sights are the 14th-century Genoese castle on **Güvercin Adası** (Pigeon Island), now housing a disco and several tearooms, and the 16th-century **Kervansaray** by the harbour, now back in service as a hotel and nightclub. There are no beaches in town, but there are several in the area: the best are Kadinlar Denizi (Ladies' Beach), to the south, and Tusan beach and Pamucak beach, a few kilometres north.

Shopping in Kuşadası

Steam buffs may want to take a trip a short distance inland to the village of Çamlık where the **Çamlık Buharlı Lokomotif Müzesi** (Locomotive Museum; daily 8.30am–5.30pm; charge) is home to some 25 pre-World War II steam locomotives.

Priene

About 33km (20 miles) to the south, the **Samsundağ Milli Parkı** (also known as the Dilek Peninsula; daily 8am–6.30pm; charge plus car park fee), a stunningly beautiful 27,000-ha (66,700-acre) national park with fine beaches, woodlands, wildflowers and rare populations of wild horses, bears and Anatolian leopards. On the flanks of Samsun Daği (Mt Samsun) itself, 37km (23 miles) from Kuşadası, **Priene** (daily 8.30am–6pm; charge) has one of the finest settings of any ancient city in Anatolia, on a series of pine-clad terraces backed by towering cliffs with views across the Menderes valley. Founded by the Greeks in the 11th century BC, with a port at the foot of the hill, this was one of the first to

silt up, before the Romans arrived, the architecture retaining its Ionian purity. There is a marked trail around the steep site, through the grid of streets, past houses and shops, council buildings, the agora, Temple of Zeus and Temple of Athena (designed by Pytheos, architect of the Mausoleum, *see page 49*), the theatre and the Sanctuary of Demeter.

Miletus and Didyma

Carry on south for another 22km (14 miles) along Route 09-55 and you reach the next of the great Greek city states that once traded along this coast, **Miletus** (Milet; Tue–Sun 8.30am–5.30pm, till 7pm in summer; charge). Settled by Minoans from Crete in the 12th century BC, it became hugely rich, with colonies in Egypt and the south of France, and was the birthplace of Thales, considered to be the first of the great Greek philosophers in the 6th century BC, noted for his rejection of hypocrisy. Relatively little of the city remains, but the huge theatre, with seating for 25,000, is in astonishing condition.

Mask of Medusa at Didyma

Nearby **Didyma** (Didim; 7km/4 miles from the main road; daily 8.30am–5.30pm; charge) is best visited at sunset when the light glows through the columns of its superb Temple of Apollo, home to one of the great oracles of the ancient world. Work on this vast marble temple, meant to have 108 columns, went on for 400 years from the 4th century BC, but was never completed. The whole surrounding area, including the tourist town of **Altınkum** 5km (3 miles) south, which has a fine beach, has been overwhelmed by building work as developers cash in on the desire of northern Europeans to own a little piece of sunshine.

Excursion to Pamukkale

These cities all once stood on the wandering delta of the Menderes River, known in classical times as the Meander (giving us the verb we still use today). Follow it inland along Route 585 to **Aphrodisias** (80km/50 miles from the coast; daily 9am–5.30pm in winter, until 7pm in summer; charge), a wonderful city devoted in antiquity to marble sculpture and the cult of love. Most of the well-restored ruins date to the 1st and 2nd centuries AD, centred on a magnificent theatre, 30-seat stadium, one of the best preserved in Anatolia, the Tetraopylon (gateway) and the Temple of Aphrodite, later converted into a Christian Byzantine basilica.

A further 90km (56 miles) inland, is one of the world's most stunning natural displays, the so-called 'cotton castle' at **Pamukkale** (daily 8am–6pm in winter, until 7pm in summer; charge), an extraordinary travertine fall with hot springs that have cascaded down the side of the hill, laying down chalk-white pools and formations that glimmer and change with the light. There is a village, Pamukkale Köyü, at the base of the plateau, but the main entrance is at the top, where you will also find the huge ruined city of **Hierapolis**, founded by Eumenes II of Pergamon, which grew rich from the wool trade and as a spa. It had a large large Jewish and later Christian community but was virtually destroyed during the early Arab invasions in the 7th century.

Only one path can be used at a time for paddling in the travertine terraces, to protect them from erosion, but take a swimming costume for a dip in the Antique Pool, the once sacred bathing area of the spa (said to be good for arthritic complaints). Most of the larger tourist hotels and many other spas are a few kilometres away in the village of Karakhayıt.

On the terraces of Pamukkale

THE TURQUOISE COAST

Bodrum

A playground for Turks and foreigners alike, this south-western corner of Anatolia, where the Aegean and the Mediterranean meet, has relatively little in the way of high culture and ancient artefacts but what it does have is stunning scenery, fabulous beaches, sybaritic party resorts and clear blue waters that make yachtsmen and divers drool.

Party central is **Bodrum**, 125km (78 miles) south of Didim. Bodrum's name means 'dungeon' and it was used as a place of exile by the Ottomans; these days, it is where the young

Bodrum by night

Istanbullus come to party to get their first taste of freedom. It is also one of the most liberal and gay-friendly towns in Turkey. The town itself has stayed fairly small and low-slung, its houses piled around the bays like sugar cubes. Nothing about it is quite as it seems. If you book a hotel here, you may well be staying in one of a dozen resort villages that encircle the twisting Bodrum pensinula, an hour's drive from town. Bodrum hardly seems to be in Turkey – it is so much richer, more sophisticated, and worldly that it would seem more at home on the Riviera. None of this may matter, but it does need to be understood when booking your holiday.

Founded in the 12th century BC as Halicarnassos, in the 4th century BC it was ruled by King Mausolus of the Carians, whose sister/wife, Artemesia, built him a tomb so grand that the **Mausoleum** (Tue–Sun 8.30am–5.30pm; charge) became one of the seven wonders of the ancient world and the tomb after which all others were named. It was nearly 50m (160ft) high, with 250,000 stones and surrounded by grand friezes, but only fragments of it now remain, and most of the best bits are in the British Museum. Just to the north is the ancient **theatre** (Tue–Sun 8.30am–5.30pm; charge), recently restored and back in use for concerts. Once seating more than 13,000, most of it was destroyed by an

Herodotus

Named the 'Father of History' by Cicero and, less flatteringly, the 'Father of Lies' by his detractors, Herodotus lived in Halicarnassos (modern Bodrum) from c.484–425BC. A keen Greek historian, he was the first person in history to collect, collate and publish his material systematically and objectively, publishing *The Histories*, a history of the 5th-century Persian Wars and strange travellers' tales reported by returning sailors.

earthquake, with the stone reused to build the castle, and the new version is a cosier 1,000 seater.

The **Castle of St Peter** (Tue–Sun 9am–5pm, but different opening times for the many halls inside; charge), built in the 15th century by the Knights of St John, is a magnificent fortress that was for years a lone, heavily fortified outpost of militant Christianity. It is now home to a world-class Museum of Underwater Archaeology, whose treasures include a 14th-century BC shipwreck in the Uluburun Wreck Hall, an 11th-century AD Byzantine ship and its cargo, in the Glass Wreck Hall, and the richly endowed tomb of a Carian Princess, whom some say might have been Artemesia herself, dating to about 360 BC.

Bodrum Resorts

An ever-increasing ribbon of hotels, apartments and villas envelop the peninsula that stretches out to the west and north of Bodrum, but the different resorts do have distinct identities. **Gümbet** is popular with party-loving youngsters from the UK, **Gumuşluk** is a relatively quiet fishing village, **Torba** is good for families, with lots of smaller hotels, **Yalıkavak** is small, calm and more suited to the slightly older market, while **Türkbükü** is a very trendy, very expensive party town. **Ortakent** and **Turgutreis** are a mass of high-rise hotels.

The Road to Marmaris

As the fish swims, Marmaris isn't that far. It is possible to go by car ferry in summer, otherwise it takes a long time to twist around the huge bays, with the road switchbacking through superb mountain scenery and scented pine forests, past small roadside stalls selling forest honey and olive oil.

Stop for a look at **Milaş**, near the airport, home to a distinctive style of carpet, some fine old Ottoman architecture and an excellent Tuesday market; and **Muğla**, the local provincial capital, its back streets still filled with wooden Ottoman houses. The huge Thursday market here is one of the best in Turkey with people pouring in from the surrounding villages.

Marmaris

In 1522, Suleyman the Magnificent anchored the entire Turkish fleet in Marmaris harbour, and in 1798 Lord Nelson rested the whole British fleet here en route to Egypt to defeat Napoleon's armada at the Battle of the Nile. The deep inlet still offers some of the best sailing territory on the coast, and is home to Turkey's largest marina. Marmaris has a small **castle** near the bazaar (one of the best places along the coast for souvenir shopping), built originally by the Knights of St John, taken over by the Ottomans and now housing an interesting

The scenic Marmaris Peninsula

The theatre at Knidos

little museum (Tue–Sun 8.30am–noon, 1–5pm; charge). On the main road into Marmaris is a new private archaeology and ethnography museum, the nicely laid out **Halici Ahmet Urkay Müzesi** (Maşhan Mevkii; Tue–Sun 9am–6pm; charge), complete with carpet and craft shops.

But most people come to Marmaris for the sun, sea, watersports and nightlife, the latter found in the town centre Bar Street, and in the resort hotels, discos and clubs that stretch out along the beaches of **İçmeler** and **Turunç** around the bay. Those looking for more peace and quiet head further out onto the remote **Bozburun Peninsula** where wonderful little boutique hotels and small villages are relatively undiscovered amidst the wild mountains and swooping hairpin bends.

Further along the peninsula, 76km (47 miles) from Marmaris, **Datça**, once a peaceful fishing village, is rapidly growing into a fully-fledged resort town in its own right, and beyond that is the area's only major archaeological site, the virtually unexcavated city of **Knidos**, once the site of a famous shrine to Aphrodite.

It is also possible to do day or overnight trips from both Marmaris and Bodrum across to the Greek island of **Rhodes,** with its fabulous Crusader castles.

Dalyan

There are a number of purpose-built, identikit resort towns all along the south coast, but it is another 75km (46 miles) to the east that you meet the next real gem, at **Dalyan**. This quiet little town lies on a reed-lined river, the Dalyan Cayı, partway between Lake Köyceğiz and the sea. There are no sites within the town itself, although there are fine views of some 4th-century BC Carian rock tombs in the cliff opposite. Most activities involve long, slow, sleepy trips on the river in one of the many boats that vie for your custom along the central quays.

Upstream **Lake Köyceğiz** is open brackish water surrounded by reed beds where kingfishers and herons fish. Up to 180 species of birds can be seen here as migrants stop to join the local residents and there are plenty of butterflies, dragonflies and other wildlife from frogs to fish (dalyan means fishing weir), including excellent grey mullet and sea bass which end up on local plates. Or you can cross over the lake to the **thermal springs** and **mud baths**, rich in minerals and radioactive elements that are meant to be great cures for a

Mud bathers at Lake Köyceğiz

raft of complaints from nervous and digestive disorders, to arthritic, skin, liver, spleen and bowel complaints, as well as increasing male potency! After coating yourself in mud or wallowing in a 40°C mud bath and soaking in the sulphur pool, you are more than ready for the next part of the day.

Downstream, the river twists its way idly down to the sea, past the ruins of ancient **Kaunos** (daily 8.30am–5.30pm; charge), first settled by the Carians of Halicarnassos in the 9th century BC. Various people owned it over the centuries leaving their mark on the architecture, from imposing Lycian rock tombs, set high to allow their inhabitants to continue socialising with their friends and neighbours, to 4th-century BC walls, a Greek theatre, and Roman baths, all swathed in thick vegetation. This isn't an easy sight to explore and many simply choose to glance as they drift past on

Turtles

Loggerhead turtles (caretta caretta) breed on 17 beaches around Turkey. The turtles mate during the spring migration, the huge females, who can weigh up to 180kg (350lb) and are about 1m (3ft) long, heaving themselves ashore at the beach where they themselves were born, any time between May and September, to lay clutches of up to 100 leathery ping pong ball-sized eggs in the hot sand. These take two months to hatch, with the hatchlings primed to head for the water by the moonlight glinting on the waves. The lights of hotels and even torches can disorientate them and kill their chances of survival as the seabirds swoop in for a feast. These days, most turtle beaches are off-limits at night in breeding season and you will see markers guarding the nests to stop you spearing them with beach umbrellas.

If they make it to adulthood (always dicey) a loggerhead will usually live well past 30 years and can survive up to 200 years. They are mainly carnivorous, living on shellfish, jellyfish and other marine life.

The Lycian rock tombs of Kaunos

their way down to **İstuzu Beach**, a superb 8-km (5-mile) long sandbar that has blocked off the lagoon, shared by happy sunbathers during the day and loggerhead turtles *(see opposite)* who heave themselves ashore by night to lay their eggs. There are strict laws protecting the nests and the beach is closed at night during nesting season.

Dalaman

Until very recently, there was virtually nothing at **Dalaman**, but a rather boring market town and a useful airport. All that is changing very rapidly, with an US$18 billion investment project that has turned the airport into the third largest in Turkey and is developing the area for tourism. By 2011, it is due to have 75,000 hotel beds and a marina, along with a variety of entertainments and activities from thermal spas to watersports, waterparks and golf courses. There are hotels along the beach at nearby **Sarıgerme**.

THE LYCIAN COAST

From Dalaman, the road stretches eastwards to Fethiye for nearly 100km (60 miles) with relatively little to excite the visitor other than the purpose-built yachting resort of **Göcek**. Then it all changes as you enter the heartland of ancient Lycia, the rugged Taurus Mountains that soar out of the sea into sharp rocky crests. Until 1981 there was no coast road and much of this area was only accessible by sea. All this has now changed but this is still probably the most spectacularly beautiful area of the whole coast as well as being one of the most historically rich.

Fethiye

The main market town for a booming region, **Fethiye** is swelling rapidly. The town, previously called Megri or Makri, was renamed Fethiye when Turkey became a republic, in honour of an airman, Fethi Bey, who crashed here. It was devastated by an earthquake in 1856, and after a further earthquake in 1957 much of it had to be rebuilt. However, there are some fine **Lycian rock tombs** in the cliff above the old town, centred around the 4th-century BC Tomb of Amyntas (take the steps from Kaya Caddesi, behind the bus station; daily 8.30am–sunset; charge) and several free-standing tombs scattered round the town. It also has a small restored classical theatre and a **museum** (off

Beach clubs

There are relatively few big beaches along this stretch of coast and many of the small inlets and coves are hard to get to. If you are not staying at a resort hotel with bathing platforms you may like to check out one of the beach clubs – a place to swim and sunbathe by day, with swimming platforms, pools, sunbeds, drinks and snacks, transforming into restaurants and dance clubs by night.

Atatürk Caddesi; Tue–Sun 8.30am–5pm; charge) filled with finds from the nearby sites. A ruined Crusader **castle** tops the hill above the town and there is an Ottoman **hammam** (Turkish bath) in the bazaar district, a perfect place to clean off the dust of the day in historic glory *(see page 95)*. There are plenty of boat trips available from the bustling harbour front; there is also an excellent market on Tuesday. The nearest beaches are in Çaliş, which also has a waterpark, Sultan's Aquacity.

Ölüdeniz

The real tourism hotspot of the region is about 15km (9 miles) south of Fethiye, centred on **Ölüdeniz** lagoon, the beach that features in almost every advertisement for the Turkish coast. It is picture-book perfect, an indigo oval fringed by white sand and backed by soaring mountains clad in richly scented pine forests. The area immediately around the lagoon has been declared a national park and is protected from development, but this is a very small area and the whole valley is filled with hotels and apartment blocks. At the top of the cliffs the next town of **Hisaronu** has grown up to feed a decidedly mass market and predominantly British tourist trade.

Beyond the sandbar, on the open water, there is a wide range of watersports on offer,

The sandbar at Ölüdeniz

and Ölüdeniz is also *the* place to go paragliding *(see page 90)*. One of the most popular local excursions is the short boat trip across to **Kelebek Vadisi** (Butterfly Valley), a steep-sided flat-bottomed valley with a waterfall at the back. Some 30 species of butterfly and 40 species of moth finding their way here in season (June–Sept). The valley is most easily accessed from the sea.

Another local attraction is the haunting ghost town of **Kaya Köyü** about 5km (3 miles) from Ölüdeniz. Originally known in antiquity as Karmylassos, this was a Greek village until the 1923 exchange of populations. The incoming Turks, convinced the houses were cursed, refused to move in and built themselves new places from scratch, leaving this eery village of some 400 small houses and two basilicas, only a handful of which have been restored. It is now a World Heritage Site. Ölüdeniz is also the start of the 500-km (310-mile) long **Lycian Way** walking trail through to Antalya *(see page 90)*.

The Eşen Valley

East of Fethiye, the coast dives south in a fat mountainous bulge. The main road cuts inland to Antalya, the far more scenic coast road turns off at

Rock tombs at Tlos

Kemer. From here, a clutch of sites line both sides of the Eşen Valley and you need two days to visit them all (one for each group). Tlos, Saklıkent and Xanthos run down the east of the valley; the much smaller Pinara and Letoön to the west. For the really keen there are a number of other small archaeological sites in the area;

there's also plenty of walking, whitewater rafting on the river, mountain biking and horse-riding available locally.

Tlos (36km/22 miles east of Fethiye; 8.30am–5.30pm; charge) was mentioned by the Hittites in the 14th century BC and was still inhabited by a notorious pirate, Kanlı Ali (Bloody Ali) in the 19th century. Built vertically on a towering rock outcrop, with the Roman city spreading out at its feet, it has some superbly carved 7th-century BC rock tombs, one supposedly the tomb of Bellerophon, slayer of the Chimaera (*see page 68*), showing him riding the winged horse, Pegasus.

River walking in the Saklıkent Gorge

Follow the back road from here through to **Saklıkent Gorge** (boardwalk daily 8.30am–6pm; charge; parking fee). Some 300m (1,000ft) high and 12km (8 miles) long, this narrow canyon in the 3,016-m (9,892-ft) Gombe Akdağı is the longest and deepest gorge in Turkey. As you come close, the road is lined with restaurants because that is the main reason people come here – to escape the heat of the coast, have a paddle or a swim in the cold mountain water and eat trout. Once you get into the national park itself, you can eat on low platforms beside the rushing waters as they cascade out of the gorge. A boardwalk offers a safe and easy stroll a short distance into the canyon.

The theatre at the Letoön

The back road carries on through to **Xanthos** (1km/ ½ mile from Kınık town; daily 8am–7pm in summer, till 6.30pm in winter; charge). This was the capital of the Lycian Federation and a place famed for its fierce pride and independence. Twice, in 540BC when besieged by the Persian general Harpagos, and again in 42BC, when attacked by Roman legions led by Brutus, the people chose to commit mass suicide rather than surrender, the warriors slaughtering their wives and families and torching the city before heading out for a final hopeless battle. Each time, sufficient numbers appear to have survived for it to have been rebuilt, as it has a large number and variety of ruins, from a Roman theatre and mosaic-decorated Byzantine basilica to numerous fine tombs. British archaeological scavenger, Sir Charles Fellows, came through here in 1842, loading his booty into a couple of Royal Navy ships (with the Sultan's permission) and many of the finest friezes, including the originals from the 5th-century BC Tomb of the Harpies and the Ionic temple known as the Nereid Monument are now in the British Museum.

Across the valley from Xanthos, the **Letoön** (daily 7.30am–7pm in summer, 8.30am–5pm in winter; charge), founded in the 7th century BC, is probably one of the prettiest of all the archaeological sites in Turkey. It was never a city but a reli-

gious sanctuary and shrine dedicated to the goddess Leto and her twin children, Artemis and Apollo. Legend has it that Leto was a nymph who, like so many before her, caught the eye of Zeus, ended up pregnant and fleeing from the anger of his jealous wife, Hera. She was befriended by wolves who brought her to this place of sanctuary. The incident also named the Lycian culture, based on the Greek lykos (wolf), and Leto became the presiding deity of the culture. She later proved to have a nifty line in vengeful behaviour, turning into frogs two shepherds who refused her a drink of water, which accounts for the large population of frogs that inhabit the sanctuary today.

There are three temples on the site, one, built in the 3rd-century BC, dedicated to Leto, one to Apollo and one to Artemis, together with an assembly ground used as the Lycian parliament and for major festivals, and a theatre.

Patara

The oracle of Apollo once lived in **Patara** (18km/11 miles south of Xanthos; daily 7.30am–7pm in summer, 8.30am–5pm in winter; charge and parking fees) although his temple is still lost beneath the copious sands. Sun worship of a different sort is the main activity these days – Patara has one of Turkey's finest beaches, a blindingly white 18-km (11-mile) long stretch of sand that has been saved from overdevelopment by the presence along much of its length of the ancient city and turtle nesting grounds, forcing the hotels inland. There is very little in the way of shade or refreshment, so take supplies.

Patara beach

Patara was the key port of the Lycian Federation, and attracted many visitors over the years, from Hannibal to St Paul, while St Nicholas was born here *(see page 65)*. The site, which has never been fully excavated, is huge and covered in constantly shifting sands, with a half-buried theatre and enormous 2nd-century AD granary.

The coast between Kalkan and Kaş

Kalkan

Thirteen kilometres (8 miles) east of Patara, the road swoops abruptly down the mountain to **Kalkan**. Once a little Greek village that clung to survival on a mix of fishing, charcoal-burning and olives, it is still one of the smallest and prettiest of the resorts on the coast, its gleaming white houses piled vertically up the narrow valley above a tiny fishing harbour, smart marina and small pebble beach. There is some nightlife, but this is a relatively quiet place that has become a favourite with slightly older people who love good local food, interesting shops, boutique hotels and *pansiyons*, history and mountain walking. There are no actual sites in town, but it makes a great base. The nearest sandy beach is 6km (4 miles) east at **Kaputaş**, a tiny cove at the head of a deep gorge, reached by a long flight of steep steps off the main road. Otherwise people swim from boats or bathing platforms anchored to the rocks.

Kaş

This tiny patch of sand, and a few other sandy coves, reached only by sea, are shared with **Kaş**, 30km (18 miles) east of Kalkan, the main town on this stretch of the coast.

View from the Crusader Castle, Kekova Island

This began life as the Hellenist port of Antiphellos, making its living exporting timber and cork oaks, and, like Kalkan, becoming a Greek fishing and farming village. Like Kalkan it attracts a slightly more sedate crowd who are more into good food than the body beautiful, but it does have some extremely good shops and restaurants and a lively bar scene in season. The setting is stunning, the curved bay and whitewashed houses standing out in stark contrast to the dark pine-clad cliffs above, while a twisting peninsula juts out into the bay, playing host to a variety of hotels, villas and apartments as it grows in popularity. The town has a small 1st-century BC theatre and a huge 5th-century BC Lycian tomb, but these are incidental to the joy of wandering the streets, browsing the shops and sampling the cafés.

Gulets fan out all along the coast on day trips. One of the most popular is to **Kekova Island** and **Simena** (Kale) for an adventure that involves scrambling up to a Crusader castle, swimming off a deserted island, peering into the crystal clear waters at a Byzantine city (drowned by a massive earthquake), and wandering on the rocks around Lycian tombs, along with a nice fish lunch. Trips also leave from Üçağız and Demre.

Demre (Myra)

Confusingly, Simena is called Kale locally and so is **Demre**, 35km (21 miles) east of Kaş (the word simply means 'castle'). Known in antiquity as Myra (after myrrh which was a popular local product, along with frankincense). Demre is another town that is beginning to transform itself, and is set to become a major resort. Meantime, it is worth a stop for two important historic sights. The first is the gloriously named **Noël Baba Kilesi** (Church of Father Christmas; daily 8.30am–4.30pm; charge), built by St Nicholas *(see below)* when he was the local bishop. The saint's body was stolen by Italian traders in 1087 and is now in the Basilica of San Nicola in Bari, Italy. The church was heavily restored by by Tsar Nicholas I of Russia in the 19th century and the frescoes were badly damaged by floods in the 1990s, but it is still immensely beautiful and a major centre of pilgrimage.

Baba Noël (St Nicholas)

Born in Patara in about AD270, Nicholas became Bishop of Myra, and was persecuted by Diocletian before attending Constantine's Council of Nicaea in AD325. A miracle-worker of renown, he is said on several occasions to have thrown a bag of gold anonymously through the window of a poor girl, giving her a dowry (the bags landed in stockings). By his death in 343, his deeds ensured him a place as one of the busiest of saints, as patron saint of prisoners, sailors, travellers, unmarried girls, pawnbrokers, merchants, children, bankers, scholars, orphans, labourers, travellers, judges, paupers, victims of judicial mistakes, captives, perfumers, thieves and murderers along with many countries and cities, chief amongst them Russia and Greece. But his biggest role was yet to come, in the transformation of the 4th-century St Nicholas to Santa Claus to Father Christmas (his jolly red uniform and long white beard added by the Coca-Cola company in the 1930s to match their logo). His feast day is 6 December.

Some of the many carved masks at Myra

About 1km (½ mile) away, are the riverside remains of Lycian **Myra** (daily 7.30am– 7pm in summer, 8am– 5.30pm in winter; charge), with a fine free-standing the-atre decorated with comedy and tragedy masks and many magnificent house tombs, some copying the wood-built houses of the living in im-pressive detail, some still even showing faint traces of their original paint.

Nearby, Hadrian built a huge granary next to the little har-bour of **Andriake**. This is now the village of **Çayağzi**, the centre of local tourism development.

Finike

From Demre, the road climbs across the Taurus Mountains to **Finike**, ancient Phoenicus, 30km (18 miles) east. It has some tourism and a nice marina but is still largely an agricul-tural town, surrounded by glasshouses filled with tomatoes and aubergines, and fields of oranges and honeydew melons, according to the season. Ancient **Limyra** (8km/5miles north; open access; free), was the 4th-century BC capital of King Pericles who founded the Lycian Federation. The Lycian and later Byzantine ruins are scattered amongst the gardens of the modern village while the hill above is laced by a vast necropolis. Amongst the most elaborate of the tombs is the free-standing 4th-century BC tomb of Catabara, near the theatre, while the tomb of Pericles, the Heroön, is right up at the top, a good 40-minute climb. The frieze shows scenes from the hero-king's life.

Olympos

If that doesn't tickle your tastebuds, carry on for another 35km (22 miles) east to **Ulupinar**, famed for its clutch of trout restaurants, where you can select your victim from the stream in front of the table and then meet him again a few minutes' later, with chips, and a little salad. From here, a winding road leads down to the villages of **Olympos** and **Çıralı**, the closest thing Turkey has to a backpacker hangout. Totally unlike every other resort along the coast, this hidden corner, with its wide bay of smoothly rounded marble pebbles, is a maze of tiny, low-cost *pansiyons*, campsites, and even treehouses with just a couple of more upmarket boutique hotels.

Olympos (daily 8.30am–6pm; charge) was an important city in the Lycian Federation, but was conquered by pirates in the 1st century BC, freed by Pompey and joined the

Exploring Olympos

Roman Empire. The peaceful ruins on the river mouth are only partially excavated and contain a rich variety of wildlife from flowers and birds to frogs and terrapins as well as Lycian tombs, a Roman theatre and baths, a Byzantine basilica, 11th- to 12th-century Genoese fortifications, and abandoned chromium mines (chrome was used for tanning leather).

At the far end of the area, beyond Çıralı, a stiff walk up the hill leads to the **Chimaera** (open access; charge), an extraordinary natural phenomenon, best seen at dusk. Living flames, fed by natural methane gas, spring from the bare rock. It is named after a mythical fire-breathing monster said by Homer to have the head of a lion, the torso of a goat and the tail of a serpent, which was slain by local hero, Bellerophon, riding the winged horse Pegasus, as a task set to win the hand of the King of Lykia's daughter. Needless to say, this became a shrine to Hephaestus (Vulcan), the god of fire, and also to Mithras, the Zoroastrian god of light. It was also used as a natural lighthouse by ancient mariners.

Tahtali Teleferik

The surrounding mountains are part of the **Beydağlar Olympos National Park,** and there are many good hiking trails. Perhaps an easier way to see the mountains however is in the coast's newest attraction, the **Tahtali Teleferik** (daily 9am–7pm in summer, 10am–6pm in winter; charge), the longest cable-car ride in Europe at 4,350m (13,500ft), and the second-longest in the world. From the base station near the Phaselis turn-off, 736m (2,415ft) above sea level, it takes nearly 10 minutes to power its way up to the summit of **Mt Tahtali** at 2,365m (7,759ft), the tallest mountain in the world that rises directly out of the sea, its distinctive cone-shape so pointed that the top had to be flattened to make space for the cable station and viewing deck. The 360° views from the top are superlative.

Phaselis

Once down, cross over and carry on down to **Phaselis**
(25km/15 miles east of Olympos; daily 7.30am–7pm in summer, 8am–5.30pm in winter; charge). With its perfect mix of ancient ruins, swimming beaches and shady pine forests, this is a great place to spend a day, and gulets arrive by the score in the morning disgorging trippers. A 7th-century BC colony of Rhodes, with the land purchased for dried fish, and citizenship sold cheaply, the locals were renowned for being unscrupulous, but they prospered, exporting timber, rose oil and perfumes, and providing a base for pirates. There are three small harbours: the fortified north harbour; the central harbour for military and small trading vessels; and the south harbour where larger vessels docked. The main street, flanked by houses, baths and a small theatre crosses between them and there are many other ruins scattered amongst the trees.

The Tahtali Teleferik

PAMPHILIA

Antalya marks the gateway between the wild beauty of the Lycian coast and the tamer plains of ancient Pamphilia. The landscape was not always like this – it was only in Byzantine times that earthquakes and silt pushed the coastline away from the mountains and silted up the harbours of the ancient cities. What it has left is a wide coastal plain with plentiful land for intensive agriculture, development and, from the tourist's point of view, lovely long sandy beaches that are ideal for paddling but scenically dull.

Antalya's spacious Konyaaltı beach

Antalya

Described by Turkish poet, Mehmet Emin Yurdakul, as 'a charming girl watching her beautiful visage in the clear mirror of the Mediterranean', Antalya has drawn paeons of praise from visitors across the centuries including Ibn Battuta and Freya Stark. According to legend, 2nd-century BC King Attalus of Pergamon chose the spot for the city because it was 'heaven on earth'. These days, Antalya is a huge city, the fourth largest in Turkey with a population of around two million and getting bigger all the time. But with its broad bay, backed by the

Taurus Mountains, snow-capped in winter, and the tiny horseshoe central harbour surrounded by the walled old city, Kaleiçi, it is still incredibly beautiful. It also has a good collection of special hotels, excellent restaurants, sophisticated clubs and bars, and excellent shopping.

The Fluted Minaret (Yivli Minare)

The town's beach area lies to the west in the modern **Konyaaltı** district, which is lined by hotels and restaurants, beach parks and entertainment. This is also the home of the **Antalya Müzesi** (Kenan Evren Bulvarı; 2km (1 mile) west of the town centre; Tue–Sun 8.30am–5pm; charge), a truly world-class museum, with many of the statues and mosaics from Perge, Aspendos and Xanthos, as well as early prehistoric items found locally, a superb selection of decorative sarcophagi, and ethnographic collections covering everything from carpets to traditional dress and carriages. Look out for the silver reliquary that once held the bones of St Nicholas.

The city's other sites are all within the walls of **Kaleiçi**, entered through **Hadrian's Gate**, a triumphal arch built when the emperor visited in AD130. Nearby are the **Saat Kulesi** (clocktower) built in 1244, although the clock was added much later, 16th-century **Mehmet Paşa Camii** (mosque) and the distinctive **Yivli Minare** (Fluted Minaret), with its decorative turquoise and blue tiles, whose adjoining mosque is now an art gallery. Write a wish and put the paper in the

Fine facilities

'There are eight bath-houses in the city, most within the walls, and a bazaar on the outskirts. Here there are twenty Muslim neighbourhoods and four Greek neighbourhoods, but the non-Muslims know no Greek. The harbour has space for two hundred ships, but since wind and gales are frequent in the harbour, the ships moor to high rocks on the shore.'

The renowned Turkish traveller Evliya Celebi, who visited Antalya in 1671–2.

ancient olive tree next to the minaret and it will come true. Further along, the **Kesik Minare** (Broken Minaret) is an all-purpose religious site that has, in its time, been a Roman temple, a Byzantine church and an Ottoman mosque. On the headland overlooking the harbour, the squat round **Hıdırlık Kulesi** may have begun life as a lighthouse in the 2nd century AD. The only museum in Kaleiçi is the **Suna-İnan ve İnan Kıraç** (Mediterranean Civilisations and Research Institute; Barbaros Mah, Kocatepe Sok 25; Thur–Tue 9am–6pm; charge), a small, private museum in a restored Ottoman mansion. The Greek church of **Agios Georgios** (St George) has collections of ceramics, archaeology and ethnography, including rooms restored as tableaux. Antalya's oldest **hammam** (bath-house) is just opposite. All around these are a maze of small steep streets and alleys filled with old Ottoman houses, many restored as hotels, restaurants and shops that make this an ideal place to stroll, stopping for an occasional glass of mint tea and some hard bargaining. Boat trips leave from the harbour.

Termessos

It takes a lot of puff to climb up to the romantically overgrown and largely unexcavated ruins of **Termessos** (the Eagle's Nest; 37km/23 miles northwest of Antalya; daily

8am–7pm; charge) which teeters precariously on the top of a crag, 1,650m (5,413ft) high in the Taurus Mountains. Even Alexander the Great gave up on the climb as its notoriously warlike citizens, who lived on olives and banditry, hurled boulders over the ramparts at his troops. For those who make the trek, the setting is incomparable, with the theatre sandwiched between a cliff and a deep gorge. It also has a large gymnasium, Odeon, temple complex and necropolis. The surrounding national park is immensely beautiful, filled with wildflowers and butterflies and has a few rare Anatolian Lynx. Nearby **Döşmealtı** village is a renowned carpet weaving centre.

The Taurus Mountains are riddled with caves and many of them have evidence of human and proto-human habitation going back millennia as well as fine stalactite and stalagmite formations. A few of them are open to the public, others can

Dramatic Termessos

Inside the Karain Cave

be visited by expert cavers. The first people started living in **Karain Mağarasi** (Karain Cave; 27km/17 miles northwest of Antalya, off the N-650 to Burdur; 6km/4 miles from the main road; daily 8.30am–5pm; charge) about 30,000 years ago, and it was someone's home for some 20,000 years, producing an invaluable stream of prehistoric evidence. It is easy to visit, with stairs, lights and a small site museum.

Perge

As you leave Antalya and head east, the main road is lined by outlet malls, discount stores and huge emporia selling everything from gold and diamonds to carpets.

The **Kurşunlu Şelalesı** (Kurşunlu Falls; 23km/14 miles east of Antalya, 7km/4miles off main road; daily 8.30am–5.30pm; charge) is a popular daytrip for families from Antalya, with a small national park with a picnic area and walks surrounding high, stepped waterfalls.

A few kilometres further on, **Perge** (daily 9am–7.30pm in summer, until 6pm in winter; charge and parking fees) is one of the most extensive and best preserved of the ancient cities in Turkey. Already thriving by the 13th century BC, it was used by Alexander the Great during his Pamphylian campaign, eventually passing to Pergamon and finally dying during the Byzantine era when its harbour silted. The impressive monuments begin on the drive towards the main site with the 14,000-seat theatre and a superbly preserved 12,000-seat stadium (both 2nd century AD). The entrance was through the giant red 3rd-century BC Hellenistic Gates from where visitors could turn left towards a series of elegant and highly sophisticated baths, right towards the 4th-century AD forum or continue straight along the colonnaded main street, its marble paving stones still clearly showing the ruts of carts and carriages, many of the shops to either side still with mosaic floors. At the far end, on the acropolis, are fragmentary remains of the earliest city. Perge is the start of the **St Paul Trail** *(see page 90).*

Twenty-five years ago, the long stretch of flat white sand beach between Perge and Aspendos was virgin territory. Now there is a whole town, **Belek**, complete with shopping malls, a long line of luxury hotels, a great many apartment blocks and – the focus for all this frenetic building – 16 world-class championship **golf courses** so far, with more coming onstream all the time. Many people who come here to stay never get further than the golf course, but most of the hotels lay on a host of other activities. They are within easy reach of Antalya and the local sights, the beaches are superb (a view shared by local loggerhead turtles, *see page 64*), and the prices are surprisingly affordable.

Kurşunlu Falls

Aspendos

Aspendos (31km/19 miles east of Perge; daily 8am–7pm in summer, 8.30am–5pm in winter; charge) was probably founded in the 12th century BC. Although now several kilometres inland, it was a port, specialising in luxuries such as gold- and silver-embroidered kilims (carpets), lemon-wood furniture, wine and horses, and once it became the property of the King of Pergamon, its wealth and status were assured. But while there are other remains here, few visit them, choosing to concentrate solely on the fabulous 15,000-seat theatre, built by the architect Xeno during the reign of Emperor Marcus Aurelius (AD161–80), and probably the finest surviving Roman theatre in the world. It seats up to 15,000, with 40 rows of marble seats divided by 10 staircases in the lower section and 21 above. A richly decorated stage wall once held marble statues, most of which are now

The theatre at Aspendos

in Antalya Museum. It is still used for an annual summer festival of ballet and opera *(see page 97)* as well as other events. Elsewhere, look out for the elegant 880-m (2,888ft) stretch of aqueduct (1st century AD) and the beautiful 13th-century Selçuk stone bridge across the Köprüçay.

Just after Aspendos, a road turns off inland climbing into the foothills of the Taurus Mountains along the Köprü river valley. After

Rafting the Köprülü Kanyon

about 43km (28 miles) a cluster of little restaurants marks the beginning of the **Köprülü Kanyon**, a stunning stretch of scenery that offers some of the country's most famous whitewater rafting, great mountain trout for fishermen and gourmets and plenty of lovely walks in the cool fresh mountain air. A single-arched Roman stone bridge crosses the gorge and a gravel road follows it, climbing ever higher to the village of **Altınkaya** (Zerk) where the ruins of ancient **Selge**, once a city of 20,000 people, are threaded amongst the cabbages and fruit trees in people's back yards in a truly spectacular setting.

Side

Pronounced Seeday and meaning pomegranate (a symbol of fertility), **Side**, 22km (14 miles) east of Aspendos, has been a holiday resort since long before Anthony and Cleopatra met up here, supposedly to negotiate a timber concession. Then it combined hedonistic pursuits with piracy and slaving, these days, it concentrates on the former. The ancient monuments are threaded through the modern resort, which is delightful out of season and, while tamer than it once was, can still be a heaving mass of alcohol-fuelled bodies in summer. Resort hotels fan out along the beaches to either side like great all-inclusive wings.

At the entrance to the town are the 17,000-seat **theatre** and the **Archaeological Museum** (Tue–Sun 9am–noon, 1–5pm; charge). Beside the harbour, perfectly positioned to catch the sunset, are the **Temples of Athena and Apollo**.

Manavgat is Side's much larger neighbour, with little to recommend it to tourists other than boat trips to the local waterfalls. From here, there are very long drives, with not a lot to entertain en route. At **Alarahan** (43km/26 miles east of Side, 9km/6 miles off the main road; daily 9am–11pm; charge) is one of the finest of some 200 Seljuk caravanserais,

Local transport on Side beach

built in about 1231 by Seljuk Sultan Alâeddin Keykubad I for travellers on the Silk Road. Set at a comfortable day's journey apart, these fabulous institutions offered lodging to travellers and their animals, along with clothes, medical assistance, baths, spiritual guidance and protection. The Sultans got the local landlords to foot the bill by tax-

Alarahan fortress

ing any who had permitted crime in their area. Today, Turkish evenings with belly dancing are held here three nights a week. An impressive Byzantine **fortress** garlands the mountain just to the north of the carvanserai.

Alanya

Alanya, 39km (24 miles) further east, stands off on its own as a resort that was until very recently an almost entirely German domain, although the Brits and Russians are now invading in search of cheaper property prices and huge sandy beaches. With its own international airport opening, this whole area, largely ignored in favour of the west so far will start to open up.

Alanya is not a particularly attractive town, with masses of mass market hotels and apartment blocks both in town and stretching out along the beaches. **İncekum**, 20km (12 miles) west of town, is the place to come if reasonably-priced sun, sand and partying is your thing. However, it does also have some history, with a fortress built by a 1st-century BC pirate chief, Diodotus Tryphon, before he was kicked out of the region by Pompey, and Coracesium, as the town was then known, joined the Roman Empire. In 44BC, Mark Anthony gave the whole region to Cleopatra. The city became Kalonoros under the Byzantines and was then renamed again by Seljuk Sultan Alâeddin Keykubad I in 1221 when he made the town his summer capital,

Near the harbour the 35-m (115-ft) **Kızıl Kule** (Red Tower; daily 10am–8pm; charge) was built in 1226 by a Syrian architect for Sultan Alâeddin Keykubad I to protect the dockyard. Inside it has five storeys, with arched galleries surrounding a huge water cistern. The tower now houses a small ethnographic museum. The main **Alanya Museum** (Azaklar Sok; Tue–Sun 8.30am–noon, 1.30–5.30pm; charge) is small but well-displayed, with a mix of history, classical art and ethnographic displays.

Nearby, **Damlataş Mağarasi** (Weeping Cave; 10am–6pm; charge) has two chambers with great stalactite and stalagmite formations, high humidity and high levels of carbon dioxide, natural ionisation and radiation that make it a supposedly great cure for asthma and rheumatism (if you sit in the cave four hours a day for 21 days).

Boat trips round the harbour are the only way to see the **Tersane**, the last remaining Seljuk dockyard in Turkey, five huge open workshops with arched roofs, built in 1227. They also offer spectacular views of the **Citadel** (Tue–Sun 9am–7pm; charge), the city's crowning glory, built onto a soaring 250m (820-ft) seacliff and surrounded by vast defensive walls with 150 bastions and 400 water cisterns. If you want to go up, there are 5km (3 miles) of hairpin bends up to the top.

FURTHER AFIELD

Beyond Alanya, you fall abruptly off the mainstream tourist map, although this may change with Alanya's new airport. For now, what beach tourism there is along this stretch of coast caters almost entirely to the Turkish and Arab markets, with only a few westerners venturing along here in search of its astonishingly rich history, which includes Hittite strongholds, Crusader fortresses and Biblical hotspots from Tarsus to Antakya (ancient Antioch), home of the first cathedral in Christianity. About 150km (90 miles) inland from the stretch of coast between Silifke and Adana is **Cappadocia**, a truly bizarre volcanic landscape, its tufa rock twisted and carved by wind and rain into 'fairy' chimneys, canyons and caves, used by man for a fabulous array of troglodytic cities and lavishly decorated **cave churches**.

To the southwest of Cappadocia, **Konya**, capital of the Seljuk Turks in the 12th and 13th centuries, was also the home of Mevlana Jelaleddin Rumi, an Afghan-born Islamic mystic who founded the Whirling Dervishes.

The fairy chimneys of Cappadocia

WHAT TO DO

SHOPPING

Turkey is one of the world's great bazaars, and standing at the junction of Europe and Asia, it has much of the best of both for sale – along with an awful lot of tat. Shopping is in Turkey is an art form, and an entertainment. Get into the right mood, and remember that however persuasive someone is and however much of their tea you have drunk, you do not have to buy. The Turks are happy to negotiate in all major currencies but you can often shave the price a little more by paying cash. On major purchases look out for shops displaying a tax refund sticker and you will be able to reclaim the VAT. Any antiquities need a clearance certificate for export.

Shopping habits are changing. There are far more fixed price stores, and out of town malls and discount outlets are springing up. But the most fun is still to be had in the bazaars, of which the best on the coast are in İzmir and Marmaris and, for purely photographic purposes, the weekly markets when the local farmers descend with their colourful heaps of tomatoes, aubergines and watermelons.

What to Buy

Carpets. If you really want a souvenir to remember, allow yourself to be persuaded into a carpet shop or two and spend a few happy hours haggling. Turkey is the original home of the knotted pile carpet, introduced by the Seljuks in the 12th century. There is a huge array of styles, techniques and designs across the country, from thick, shaggy Çanakkale carpets to the soft colours and floral motifs of Milaş near

Reflections in Bodrum harbour

Bodrum or the earthy geometric designs of Doşmealtı near Antalya. Finest of all are the intricate floral patterns and smooth silks of the Imperial Court carpets from Hereke. Also look out for kilims (flat-weaves) which have been produced here for at least 7,000 years, *cicims* which have designs like embroidery stitched into them, and *sumaks*, kilims from the far east with an overlay of figurative stitching.

Give yourself time to look around and gauge prices before committing yourself; perhaps have a look at one of the state-run fixed price shops or weavers' cooperatives which also give demonstrations of carpet-making.

Fashion. Turkey's textile industry is huge and many of the world's top designers make their clothes here. The result is an excellent three-tier shopping market – real designer gear in chic Bodrum, Antalya and İzmir boutiques, end of run designer gear in outlet malls outside the major towns, and a thriving – and highly illegal – trade in high-quality fakes. Off

How to Buy a Carpet

A good Turkish carpet is an expensive purchase and it can be a mine-field – are the materials and dyes natural or synthetic, how many knots are there, is it actually old or has it been aged with the help of tea and strong sunlight? The rule of thumb is that natural is best, with silk best of all, then silk/cotton, wool/cotton. Dyes should be natural and not synthetic, although many of the new synthetics are so good they have lost the brassy edge. Traditionally, every village had its own designs and every design told a story. These days more carpets are made to suit foreign tastes and the old traditions are vanishing. If you buy a genuine antique, you will need an export certificate from the Ministry; the dealer should be able to arrange it for you. Most dealers will also arrange postage, although it is surprising how the price drops if you take it with you.

Carpets from Milaş

the designer treadmill, look at the silk scarves and pashminas, thick, cuddly cotton bathrobes or made to measure clothes from a tailor in the bazaar.

Leather. The leather market is overwhelmed by fake designer bags (some of excellent quality), but Turkey produces masses of fine leather at surprisingly reasonable prices. If you want a new bag, belt, wallet, jacket, or even sandals this is definitely the place to shop. Many shops also offer a custom-design 'made-to-measure' service, offering you the coat of your dreams delivered to your hotel. Check the quality and price as both can vary hugely.

Other Great Buys. Jewellery can be a steal with delicate filigree and pieces custom-made to your own designs in the big warehouses near the major archaeological sites; gold and silver are sold by weight, with only a small premium for workmanship. Ceramics follow traditional patterns from the famous İznik tiles and the antique shops are full

Blue beads

The ubiquitous blue glass beads *(Nazar boncuğu)* are a traditional amulet designed to ward off the evil eye. Any bad luck is directed into the bead which will break once its work is done.

of lovely old copper and tin. For 'little presents', the best options are *lokum* (Turkish Delight), herbal teas, olive oil soap and spices; inlaid chess sets and backgammon boards; meerschaum pipes and carpet slippers; and of course, lucky blue beads, to ward off evil eye.

ENTERTAINMENT

There is plenty of evening entertainment all along the coast, but the vast majority of it is in the resort hotels, which lay on extravagant shows, films, belly-dance evenings, casinos, and glittering cabarets as well as pulsating nightclubs for their guests. Most also open to non-residents. Outside the hotels the streets of the resort towns are lined with bars while the larger resorts all sport a collection of noisy clubs and discos, some of which have achieved international stardom. However, almost all this frenzy of activity is only open in season (May/June–Sept). For the rest of the year, much of the coast is ghostly quiet, the domain of a few local restaurants and *çay* shops (teashops).

The exceptions to the rule are İzmir and Antalya, which are both major cities with a full local cultural programme, including resident symphony orchestras. Both have film festivals, while Aspendos, near Antalya also hosts a ballet and opera festival in the magnificent Roman theatre *(see page 97)*. But if you really want to be Turkish for an evening, search out one of the backstreet *meyhanes*, and join the locals eating meze, drinking rakı and listening to soul-wrenching *faşıl* singers.

Nightclubs

Antalya. Club Arma, Yatlimanı 42, Kaleiçi, tel: 0242-244 9710, www.clubarma.com.tr. Chic open-air dance club and restaurant by the marina, with some of the best food in town as well as the most beautiful people.

Bodrum. Halikarnas, Cumhuriyet Caddesi 178, tel: 0252-316 8000, www.halikarnas.com.tr. Internationally renowned open-air disco with world-class DJs and huge crowds.

Çeşme. Babylon, Çark Plajı, Liman Mevkii Alaçatı-Çeşme, tel: 0232-716 6707, www.babylon-alacati.com. Istanbul's most famous club has opened a branch near İzmir, attracting the same mix of international artists, with added sand, sea and palm trees.

Marmaris. Marmaris Beach Club, Uzunyalı, tel: 0252-412 1188. All day and night beach club, sun loungers by the beach to cocktails and rock at 2am.

Halikarnas in Bodrum

On the beach at Side

ACTIVE PURSUITS

Most of the large hotels have gyms and pools and many have tennis courts. The largest resorts run regular classes in everything from martial arts and aerobics to yoga.

Belek, near Antalya *(see page 75)*, was purpose-built as a world-class golfing centre with 16 championship courses and more being built every year.

Sailing and Yachting

Yachting is increasingly popular, with sleek marinas in many of the resorts; the tourist office can give you details of facilities and fees *(see page 126)*. Currents and winds along the coasts can be strong.

One of the best ways of seeing the coast is on a 'blue cruise'. The traditional wooden **gulets** sleep anything from six to 30, come with engines, sails and a staff. You can wander at will, anchoring in small bays and off islands to snorkel and sunbathe in deserted coves, arrive at coastal archaeological sites by boat and drop into the main resorts for some shopping therapy and a restaurant meal. Either arrange your trip ahead of time through operators such as Anatolian Sky (tel: 0845-365 1011, www.anatolian-sky.co.uk), Sunsail (tel: 01705-222 222, www.sunsail.com), Day Dreams (tel: 01884-849200, www.turkishcruises.co.uk) and Top Yacht (tel: 01243-520 950, www.top-yacht.com) in the UK, or ask travel agents or along the quay in the resorts.

Watersports

On this hugely long coast, there is every possibility for messing about on, in, above or below the water. The largest resort hotels have their own watersports facilities, the rest all have tie-in deals with the operators in the towns. If serious about watersports, it is probably best to look at the stretch of coast between Bodrum and Antalya, where the wilder coastline and steeply shelving shore offers better opportunities for everything from **diving** to **windsurfing** and **sailing**.

There are large areas close to the coast where it is illegal to dive because of the presence of underwater antiquities, so it is best to work with a reputable local dive school rather than branching out on your own. You can also get more information from the Turkish Diving Federation, Ulus Ishane, A. Blok., 303–304, Ulus, Ankara (tel: 0312-310 4136, fax: 0312-310 8288, www.diveturkey.com and www.scubaturkiye.com).

Inland, the Köprülü Canyon offer opportunities for kayaking and **whitewater rafting**, and the Saklıkent Gorge is great for **river walking**.

Other Activities

As well as the many sightseeing tours around the archaeological monuments and villages along the coast, there are

Divers' delights

Divers can find plenty to entertain them, from marble columns, deposited by ancient earthquakes, to Roman amphorae and a wide variety of sealife ranging from moray eels and loggerhead turtles to groupers, sardines, stingrays, barracudas, sea bream, rainbow wrasse, damsel fish, bonita, sea mullet, starfish, octopus, and dolphins.

plenty of opportunities for outdoor activities from **hot air ballooning** in the Köprülü Canyon area near Side; paragliding, especially from 1,975-m (6,480-ft) high Mt Babadaği, above Ölüdeniz; **jeep safaris**, **horse-riding**, quad-biking, **canyoning** and **rock climbing**, the length and breadth of the Taurus mountains.

Although there are plenty of good areas for **walking**, there are two particularly fine hiking trails near the south coast – the Lycian Way, which trails through the Taurus mountains from Ölüdeniz to Antalya; and the St Paul Trail, which has two branches, one starting in Perge, the other at Aspendos, which join at the Roman site of Adada before heading west to Yalvac, northeast of Lake Eğirdir. Each is about 500km (300 miles) long. English-language guidebooks are available in most Mediterranean resorts; see also www.lycianway.com.

Less energetically, there are rich **birdwatching** areas behind Belek *(see page 75)*; and in the reedy Lake Köyceğiz, near Dalyan *(see page 53)*. Further afield and inland, the freshwater marshes of Sultan Sazlığı, southeast of Cappadocia, teem with freshwater and marine species, permanent inhabitants and migrants clustering to build up an impressive list of up to 250 species. For information, contact: Doğal Hayatı Koruma Derneği (National Wildlife Protection Association), Büyük Postane Cad. Nos 43–45. Kat: 5–6, Bahçekapı 34420, Istanbul (tel: 0212-528 2030, fax: 0212-528 2040, www.dhkd.org).

Tour Operators

Antalya Balloon, Belek Tourism Centre, tel: 0242-715 1408, www.antalyaballoons.com. Soar at dawn across the landscape in a hot-air balloon.

Dragoman Outdoor Activities Centre, Uzunçarşı Caddesi 15, Kaş, tel: 0242-836 3614, www.dragoman-turkey.com. A whole range of activities from diving and sea-kayaking to mountain biking and hiking.

Kardak Tourism, Çarşı İçi, Mevkii-Dalyan, tel: 0252-284 5374, fax: 0252-284 3957, www.kardaktourism.com. Boat tours, sailing, turtle-watching, fishing, rafting, jeep safaris, hammams and even trips to Rhodes from this general purpose tour operator.

Medmar Turizm, İskele Meydanı K:2 41, Marmaris, tel: 0252-413 0406. General travel agency offering a range of local sightseeing tours and excursions.

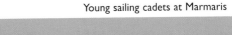

Young sailing cadets at Marmaris

Shooting the Köprülü rapids

Medraft, Yeşilbahçe Mah. Portakal Çiçeği Bulvarı Hüseyin Kuzu Ap.14/3, Antalya, tel: 0242-312 5770, fax: 0242-312 1062, www.medraft.com. Whitewater rafting in the Köprülü Kanyon; jeep safaris; cycling; gullet trips; and hiking.

Kalkan Dive Centre, Kalamar Beach, Kalkan, tel: 0532-553 2006, www.kalkandiving.com. Beginners' dives, courses and trips for experienced divers off islands, reefs and walls in the Kalkan area.

Pamfilya, Işıklar Caddesi 57/B, Antalya, tel: 0242-243 1500, fax: 0242-247 1400, www.pamfilya.com.tr. One of Turkey's largest agencies with branches in many towns, offering a wide variety of local sightseeing tours.

Trooper Tours, Akbıyık Caddesi 15, Sultanahmet, Istanbul, tel: 0212-516 9024, www.troopertours.com. Specialist day and weekend tours to Gallipoli from Istanbul.

Spectator Sports

Turkey is football mad. Every major town has a team. The country's three giant international teams are all in Istanbul, but if you want to catch a game, there are plenty around. There are also a number of more esoteric spectator sports such as oil wrestling (with the competitors greased up with olive oil), which is mainly based in European Turkey, although there are matches elsewhere; camel wrestling, which is a feature of Muğla, İzmir and Antalya provinces in February and March; and *cirit*, traditional jousting on horseback from eastern Turkey.

BATHS AND SPAS

Forget your soothing whalesong, candles and dim lights – a **hammam** (Turkish bath) is much more robust. This is designed to get you clean. It is a slice of history, the direct descendant of the Roman bath. It is also totally invigorating, makes you feel wonderful, and is a completely traditional Turkish experience. Many hotels have their own hammams but the larger cities also have traditional baths that have been operating for hundreds of years, and cost a fraction of the price.

If you want the whalesong, however, there is plenty of that on offer as well. Most of the five-star hotels and many of the smaller boutique hotels have spas while some, such as the Six Senses Spa at the Kempinski Barbaros Bay in Bodrum (see page 131) are running world-class destination spa resorts.

Bathers at Pamukkale

As a country with a considerable amount of geothermal activity rumbling away beneath its surface, Turkey also has a plentiful supply of mineral-rich **hot springs** and **mud pools** and alongside these is a healthily growing trade in **health spas** where wellness centres that offer aroma therapy massages and facials for stressed-out executives are joined by full-blown medical spas. There are several pockets around the coast – at Çanakkale, Balcova and Çeşme, near İzmir, on the Aegean Coast; on Lake Köyceğiz near Dalaman; and inland at Pamukkale.

Damlataş Aqua Center, Saray Mah., İsmet Hilmet Balcı Caddesi 62, Alanya, tel: 0242-519 1585, www.alanyahamami. com. Daily 6am–midnight. A new traditional hammam, run by the same people as Istanbul's famed Çemberlitaş Baths. Shuttle service from local hotels.

Balçova Agamemnon Thermal Baths, Hüseyin Öğütçen Caddesi 2, Balçova, İzmir, tel: 0232-259 0102, fax: 0232-259 0829. Standing on the site of the Baths of Agamemnon, supposedly used by the Greek commander for treating soldiers wounded during the siege of Troy, this is the flagship of the Turkish Government's medical spas, with a huge capacity.

Cevat Sakir Caddesi, Fabrika Sok 42, Bodrum, tel: 0252-313 4129, www.bodrumhamami.com.tr. Daily 6am–midnight. A traditional 500-year-old hammam, beautifully restored. Shuttle service from local hotels.

How to Have a Turkish Bath

Your Turkish bath starts in the reception area (camekân) where you undress, are given a locker, a sarong (peştamal), a towel and wooden clogs (takunya). You can keep on your underwear or go nude beneath the sarong – whichever makes you feel comfortable. Most baths are separated by sex, although a very few in tourist areas offer mixed bathing. You then go through to the domed main chamber (hararet), a hot steam room, with a large marble slab (gobek tasi) surrounded by small alcoves with taps of hot and cold water. Wash yourself down and stretch out in the heat to steam and get scrubbed down. This involves a rough exfoliating camel-hair glove (kese), large quantities of soap suds and buckets of water. A full body oil massage is usually an optional extra before you relax with the ubiquitous cup of tea.

Old Turkish Bath, Hamam Sokak 2, Paspatur Bazaar, Fethiye, tel: 0252-614 9318, www.oldturkishbath.com. Daily 7am–midnight. Unusually, both single-sex and mixed facilities are available at this 16th-century hammam in the bazaar area.

SPA Hotel Thermemaris, Incebel mevkii 48770 Dalaman–Muğla, tel: 0252-694 8334, fax: 0252-6948364, www.thermemaris.com. Not a great location (next to the runway of Dalaman airport) but this is a serious spa resort

Cooling of at Olympos on the Lycian Coast

with mud pools, thermal springs, and medical staff on site.

Sultaniye Natural Hot Springs and Mud Baths, Köyceğiz, Dalyan, tel: 0252-266 7778. Day baths visitable by boat from Dalyan. Take an old swimming costume.

CHILDREN'S TURKISH COAST

Turkey is a great place to take children on holiday, although it is probably sensible to avoid the heat of high summer if possible. The country is very child-friendly, hygienic, with good medical facilities. Most supplies are freely available in the resorts although you may want to take your tried and tested brands of bottled baby food and formula with you. Make sure you take hats and high factor sunblock, and give them lots of liquids. The food is relatively simple, healthy and delicious and it's easy to persuade children to eat things such as *kofte* (mini hamburgers) and chips.

For those with younger children, there are many hotels with kids' clubs and baby-sitting services. If you want a shallow, sandy beach, it is probably better to look on the Aegean Coast or between Antalya and Alanya (although Ölüdeniz and Patara also have wonderful beaches). If the children are a little older and looking for watersports, hiking and sightseeing, consider the wilder Lycian Coast between Fethiye and Antalya.

As for entertainment – beyond the hotel, the kids' club and the beach – is a whole world of excitement, from caves such as the Karain Cave near Aspendos *(see page 74)* with their towering stalactites, to horse riding in the Taurus Mountains near Olympos, and scrambling across the ruins of ancient cities.

Kids in the Saklıkent Gorge

There are also **waterparks** of various shapes and sizes scattered through the resorts along the coasts, headed by the vast Adaland in Kuşadası (tel: 0256-618 1252, www. adaland.com); which is the largest waterpark in Europe, with rides, an ocean park and a dolphinarium. Aqualand and Dolphinland, just behind Konyaaltı Beach in Antalya (tel: 0242-249 0900, www.beachpark.com.tr), also have a dolphin show and offer the opportunity to swim with the dolphins. There are other smaller parks in child-friendly resorts such as Marmaris and Alanya, with more springing up all the time.

Festivals and Seasonal Events

January *Selçuk*: Camel Wrestling Festival.

February *İzmir*: camel wrestling.

April *İzmir*: International İzmir Film Festival – new films from Turkey and elsewhere; *Gallipoli*: 25 April sees ceremonies for Anzac Day, in memory of the Australian and New Zealand troops who died here.

May *Marmaris*: International Yacht Festival; *Silifke*: Music and Folkore Festival.

June *Aspendos*: International Opera and Ballet Festival – major international stars perform in the ancient theatre; *Kaş*: Lycia Culture and Art Festival; *Alanya*: International Beach Volley Championships.

June–July *İzmir and Marmaris*: festivals of dance and music – celebrate local folk arts; *Çeşme*: Çeşme International Song Contest.

July *Antalya and Aspendos*: International Folk Festival.

August *Troy*: Troy recaptures its ancient glory with readings from Homer and a beauty contest in which a modern Helen is selected; *İzmir*: İzmir International Fair celebrates local culture.

September *Antalya*: International Akdeniz Song Contest *Marmaris*: Marmaris Tango Festival.

October *Antalya*: Altın Portakal (Golden Orange) Film Festival, celebrating the work of Turkish film makers; *Bodrum*: International Bodrum Cup – yacht race that attracts entrants from around the world. Alanya: International Triathlon Competition (swimming, cycling and running).

November *Marmaris*: International Yacht Race – Turkey's last sailing competition of the season; nationwide, 10 November: anniversary of the death of Atatürk.

December *Demre*: International St Nicholas Symposium – honours St Nicholas, the local saint (Santa Claus) whose feast day is 6th December.

Turkey also celebrates several moveable Muslim festivals each year, chief amongst them the month-long fast of **Ramazan**. Tourist restaurants remain open, but be discreet about eating and drinking in public. Dusk sees the start of a huge meal. The end of Ramadan is celebrated by the three-day Şeker Bayramı (Sugar Festival).

EATING OUT

Like the Turks themselves, Turkish cuisine is robust in attitude and irresistible in essence. One of the reasons for visiting Turkey is to indulge in the healthy, fresh food choices in authentic surroundings, rather than hotel restaurants. One should sample as many dishes as possible at different restaurants, *pide*, pudding and patisserie salons, and *kebap* places. The epitome of Turkish hospitality is sipping a glass of tea in the distinctive tulip shaped glasses.

Etiquette

From May to October, many restaurants open at breakfast and stay open until midnight or the last customer departs. Set meal times are rare except in snazzy, up market eateries. Impulse eating is a national trait.

Children are welcomed in all restaurants. A blanket ban on smoking in public places is little enforced, restaurants included. Some restaurants and smaller cafés have separate seating areas for families or women but less so in holiday resorts.

Hygiene and cleanliness are pillars of Islam and restaurants are generally scrupulously clean. You can always peek into the kitchen when you get up to select your *meze* (starter) course.

Fixed price meals are largely a tourist phenomenon but may be found on luncheon menus.

Where To Eat

Turks nibble and munch in an impressive collection of restaurants, *bufés*, kiosks, salons and bars and coffee houses. They all have different functions and here is what to expect.

A *lokanta* is the main type of restaurant found all over Turkey. Less frequently known as a *restoran*, a gastronomic range of salads, grills and starters are offered. Daily specials may be written on a board. Adventurous chefs are increasingly part of the *lokanta* scene.

A tavern *(meyhane)* is a boisterous restaurant serving Turkish specialities accompanied by quantities of liquor and poignant music and songs. More usually found in urban areas, they have a touch of the honky-tonk but guarantee a rewarding evening.

A *pastahane* (or *pastanesi*) is a patisserie with tempting showcases of biscuits, chocolate, cakes, sweet and savoury rolls and *pasta*, the general name for the sugary *baklava* and other gooey delicacies. You can usually sit at a table and have tea or coffee.

A *kahvehane* is a coffee house for men, and women are not welcome. If you see a *birahane* this is a spit and sawdust public house for men. Visit a *şaraphane* (wine bar), however, and

Waterfront restaurant at Ayvalık

Simit **bread rings**

you find slick service and excellent food with a comprehensive wine list and nibbles.

A *pide salonu* (pide salon) turns out fresh-baked flat bread (like pitta) from a wood-fired oven, with a range of delicious toppings. Many now also offer freshly-cooked main meals and may serve liquor.

A *muhallebi* sells custard puddings with rice (*sütlaç*, *kazandibi* or *keşkül*) and chocolate pudding or the divine Noah's Pudding with pulses *(aşure)*, or delicate profiteroles. You can sit at small tables or buy to take out.

Kiosks, or *bufés* are found at roadsides everywhere selling convenience foods, snacks or Turkey's tasty grilled cheese sandwich *(tost)*. Some, like the ones that line Antalya's Beach Park, are more like mid-town wine bars and brasseries.

Meals on wheels, or *sokak yemekleri* are moveable feasts that satisfy local eat-on-demand urges. Roasted chestnuts in winter are glorious but in high summer, mussels, almonds and foods containing mayonnaise may be past their pavement date.

A *simithane,* or bun shop, is a cheerful addition to Turkish eateries (a *simit* is a sesame-seed round bread ring, tasty with cream cheese, jam or just about anything). A growing trend, these places are crowded with effervescent youth.

The traditional *döner kebapı salonu* serves lamb or chicken drizzling on a revolving vertical spit. The meat is shaved off and served in *pide* (pitta) bread with garnish. It is a nourishing and economical meal, eaten in or as a take away *(paket servisi)*.

What to Eat

The stars of Turkish cuisine are less the Ottoman 'palace' dishes or the revolving roasted meat, *döner kebap*, or its cousin on a skewer, *şiş* (shish) *kebap*. Unfailingly delicious are the grand array of appetisers, known as *meze*, that introduce a typical meal in a restaurant *(lokanta)*. You either choose these yourself or, in a smart restaurant, they will be brought to your table. Typical choices are the piping hot cheese rolls *(sigara böreği)*, smoky-flavoured aubergine purée *(patlıcan salatası)*, or stuffed vine leaves *(dolması)*. Cool off with *haydarı*, a yoghurt and garlic dip. Sophisticated specialities run to shredded chicken and walnuts, *çerkez tavuğı*, and Albanian liver, *Arnavut çiğer*.

It is easy to overload on kidney beans *(barbunya)*, cheese-filled grilled mushrooms, *(mantar)*, chickpea purée *(hummus)* or the tangy compote of pickles *(turşu)*. A salad and *mezes* on their own make a colourful and flavour-filled meal.

Sweet Teeth

Syrupy pastries like *baklava* are consumed with tea or coffee, usually mid morning or during the afternoon. But Turks also love the putty-like ice cream that originated in central Anatolian Kahramanmaraş and is named after the town, *Maraş Dondurması*. It uses *sahlep* (ground orchid root) as a base, which makes it, quite literally, elastic.

Turkish delight, *lokum*, was the confection creation of an Istanbul sweetmaker, Haci Bekir, in the early 19th century. Highly prized by women of the harem, it is an ideally Turkish gift to take home – as is the rich and gritty sesame treat, *helva*.

Künefe is a special kind of cream cheese baked with shredded wheat dough and sugar syrup from the Antakya region. A dessert or snack to die for, it often has *kaymak* (clotted cream) blobbed on top.

If you are invited to dinner with a Turkish family, delight your hosts with the best selection of chocolates you can afford.

A plate of *meze*

Menus always feature fresh salads. Shepherd's salad (*çoban salatası*), for example, is finely chopped tomatoes, parsley and onions. But ask for something special, or a side dish of greens and lettuce, and they will oblige.

Main dishes are grilled chicken (*tavuk*), steak or lamb chops (*pirzola*). These come complete with garnish and rice (*pilav*), often with chips as well. On the menu you will also see stews (*güveç*), simmered or oven-baked. These are made with meat or vegetables or seafood. Aubergine is a staple food, grilled, stewed, stuffed and roasted or as a *kebap*. The Ottoman court kitchens prided themselves on having 150 recipes for this ubiquitous essential.

Fresh fish (*balık*) is a traditional meal, usually sold by weight. Always agree the price beforehand, as the final bill may surprise you. Even if you are by the sea, most fish will not be caught locally. Trout (*ala balık*) and gilt-headed bream (*çipura*) are invariably from fish farms.

Snacks and other meals

Less formal meals consist of *pide*, *lahmacun*, Italian-style pizza and *gözleme*. *Pide* is an elongated dough topped with cheese, minced meat, egg or other choices and baked in a traditional wood-fired oven. *Lahmacun* is often called Turkish pizza but the dough is more delicate and the meat and tomato topping a little spicier. *Gözleme* is a crêpe filled with cheese, onion or parsley and cooked over a griddle, or *saç*, and *ayran* (buttermilk) is its partner in thirst.

Even if a Turks sleeps into the afternoon, breakfast is obligatory. Here you find cheeses, eggs, tomatoes, cucumbers, olives and slabs of fresh crusty bread or cake. There will be butter and jams or honey. Tea is the ritual drink at breakfast. Brunch is creeping into the domain of Turkish cuisine. Brunch at a rural restaurant will have all the trappings and be filled with local people tucking into a leisurely weekend.

Beverages

Turkey is an overwhelmingly Muslim country but Turks have a relaxed tolerance to alcohol particularly in tourist venues. As you move eastwards, mini bars stock less strong drink, although every town has restaurants where alcohol can be consumed. A hefty government tax slaps a *premier cru* price tag on a cheap plonk and a bottle of wine easily doubles the cost of a budget meal.

Turkey offers reasonable, and some outstanding, domestic wines (Corvus, Sarafin and Villa Doluca are amongst the better labels) and the locally-brewed Efes and Marmara beers are a refreshing summer tonic.

Tea for two

The delightful ritual of Turkish tea drinking launches lasting friendships. It is offered generously and ubiquitously and it is impolite to refuse. If it's too strong and too sweet, ask for *Açık çay, şeker sis* (weak tea without sugar).

Turkey's national drink, *Rakı*, is an aniseed flavoured liquor distilled from a special grape variety. It is high proof and an acquired taste but goes well with many foods.

Soft Drinks (Meşrubat)

Brand-name soft drinks are found all over Turkey, as well as local upstarts like Kola Türk. Fresh fruit juices, once pulpy and wholesome, are now watery, sugary and reconstituted. Ask for a freshly-squeezed orange juice *(taze portakal suyu)* instead. Smoothies and shakes puréed from fresh or exotic fruits are a refreshing alternative. Natural mineral water *(memba suyu)*, still or sparkling, is widely available.

To Help You Order...

Do you speak English?	**Inglizce biliyormusunz?**
Waiter!	**Lütfen bakar mısmız!**
What would you recommend?	**Ne tavsiye edersiniz?**

To Help You Read the Menu...

Meze (Starters)

beyaz penir	goat's cheese
borek	pastry filled with cheese and herbs
cacık	yogurt with cucumber and garlic
çoban salatası	a salad of tomato, cucumber, peppers, onions and parsley
dolması	stuffed vine leaves
haydarı	yoghurt and garlic dip
imam bayıldı	aubergines stuffed with tomato and onion
mucver	courgette pancake
tarama	yogurt with caviar and garlic

Et (Meat)

döner kebab — sliced roasted lamb
iskender kebab döner — kebab drenched in yogurt
karısık ızgara — mixed grill
piliç — roast chicken
pitzola — lamb chops
şiş kofte — grilled lamb meatballs

Balık (Fish)

ahtapod	octopus	**kalkan**	turbot
alabalık	trout	**karide**	prawns
barbunya	red mullet	**kiliç**	swordfish
hamsi	anchovies	**midye**	mussels
kalamar	squid	**sardalya**	sardines

Sebze (Vegetables)

bakla	broad beans	**lahana**	cabbage
bamya	okra	**nohut**	chickpeas
domates	tomatoes	**patates**	potatoes
ispanak	spinach	**patlıcan**	aubergine

Tatlı (Dessert)

dondurma — ice cream
kadayıf — shredded wheat in syrup
kadın göbeği — doughnut in syrup
keşkül — vanilla almond custard
lokum — Turkish delight
pasta — pastry or cake
sütlac — rice pudding

Beverages

bira — beer
çay — tea
kahve — coffee

HANDY TRAVEL TIPS

An A–Z Summary of Practical Information

A

ACCOMMODATION

The Turkish coast has a huge number of hotels, of every conceivable shape and size.

So many new hotels are opening here that anything built more than 10 years ago is considered old. The good news is that as the coast matures the boxy concrete mass market hotels that led the charge are gradually being joined or replaced by some far more exciting properties, including an interesting array of restored historic houses, delightful small boutique hotels and pensions *(pansiyons)*, eco-resorts, spas, and some extremely luxurious five-star de-luxe resorts. The bad news is that concentration is often on building great facilities with less care put into upkeep or restoration, so quality can drop as the building ages. An excellent website for attractive small hotels is www.nisanyan.net. Exclusive Escapes tel: +44 (0)20-8605 3500, www.exclusiveescapes.co.uk is a UK-based tour operator working with some of the finest small hotels along the coast.

There is a star rating system, based entirely on the number of amenities offered (en-suite bathrooms, lifts, etc.) and some of the most delightful hotels are not rated or are classified as 'special', as they are in historic properties, or may offer five-star service but are in small buildings and out of the way locations and are unable to

I have a reservation.	**Reservasyonim var.**
I'd like a single/double room.	**Tek/çift yataklı bir oda istiyorum.**
With shower	**Duşlu**
What is the price per night?	**Bir gecelik oda ücreti ne kadar?**
Can I see the room?	**Bakabilimiyini?**

offer the technical trimmings. If you have any physical disabilities, always check on access, as much of the area is extremely steep and you may have to negotiate a lot of stairs. Many hotels along the coast open only between late April and October. If travelling out of season, check that your hotel has year-round hot water and central heating, as many use solar heating.

With recent changes allowing foreigners to own property there is also an increasing range of self-catering property available to rent in the main resorts, via websites such as www.holidaylets.net, www.holidaylettings.co.uk, www.ownersdirect.co.uk and www. holiday-rentals.co.uk.

Tourist information offices *(see page 126)* can provide a list of accommodation but few offer any descriptions or are prepared to recommend one property over another.

AIRPORTS *(havalimani*; see also GETTING THERE)

Air travellers are spoiled for choice with airports scattered right along the coast. İzmir, Dalaman, and Antalya all have scheduled services from a variety of European cities year-round, served by both mainstream and low-cost airlines. In summer, the charter flights kick in with huge numbers of additional services to Bodrum. A new international airport was due to come onstream at Alanya at the time of writing, with the promise of involvement from low-cost airlines.

B

BICYCLE AND MOPED HIRE

There aren't a great many hire outlets, but most adventure tour operators offer mountain biking and many hotels have mountain bikes for guests. Most resorts have at least one outlet where you can hire mopeds and scooters. You will need a driver's licence. Make sure rates include insurance, and insist on being given a helmet.

BUDGETING FOR YOUR TRIP

Turkey has been selling itself very successfully as the cheap destination outside the euro zone, but prices have risen sharply in recent years and while it is still good value, it is not ultra-cheap. Accommodation is reasonably priced, although notably more expensive in İzmir, Bodrum and Antalya than along the rest of the coast. Prices start at around US$80 a night for a good pension, ranging up to US$400 a night for a luxury 5-star hotel in one of the major cities. Car hire is not exorbitant, but fuel is astronomically expensive (diesel is cheaper than petrol) at over US$2 a litre. Local transport is very cheap.

You can eat extremely cheaply if you are prepared to go off the tourist standard into the backstreet kebab shops and the roadside *gözleme* stalls, but in normal restaurants expect a meal for two (without alcohol) to start at around YTL80. Fish is considerably more expensive than meat. Coffee is more expensive than tea, but both are cheap, unless you start indulging in cappucinos which can run to London-style prices of YTL10. Imported alcohol is several times the price of the local brew. A 1 litre bottle of water will cost you YTL2 in a corner shop and up to YTL15 in a restaurant or hotel.

C

CAMPING *(kamping)*

There are very few camping and caravan sites and facilities tend to be somewhat rudimentary. Some pensions and rural hotels allow camping in their grounds and there are campsites along the Lycian Way (www.lycianway.com). Local tourist offices can usually provide a list of facilities, including those managed by the forestry department, national park service and other government agencies, or contact the Turkiye Kamp ve Karavan Dernegi (Turkish Camp and Caravan Association, Bestekar Sok No. 62/12 Kavaklidere, Ankara, tel: 0312-466 19 97, fax: 0312-426 85 83, www.kampkaravan.org).

CAR HIRE

All the major international car hire companies have outlets at the main airports and there are also plenty of large and small Turkish companies to choose from. Rates start at around US$500 per week.

To hire a car, you must be over 21 and have held a licence for at least a year. Look for a deal that includes mileage and Collision Damage Waiver. Insurance4CarHire (tel: 020-7012 6300, www.insurance4carhire.com) is an excellent annual scheme that insures your CDW excess and can save a fortune in additional premiums abroad. The credit card used will need to be in the driver's name. Tax is added to all car rentals, and a surcharge may be applied if you want a one-way rental or ask for the car to be delivered or picked up from your hotel. If you need a child seat, order it on booking; and check that you have a full set of spares and a proper spare tyre (punctures are common).

NB: insurance claims are invalid unless accompanied by a police report so if you do have an accident, notify the police immediately, or the agency is allowed to charge you for damages even if you have taken out insurance.

Avis: www.avis.co.uk, tel: 0844-581 0147; **Budget:** www.budget.co.uk, tel: 0844-581 9998; **Hertz:** www.hertz.co.uk, tel: 08708-448844; **Europcar**: www.europcar.co.uk, tel: 08706-075000; **Thrifty-Decar:** www.decar.com.tr, tel: 444 3 227; **Sixt Rent a Car:** www.sixt.com, tel: +90 (232) 444 0076.

CLIMATE

There are several hundred kilometers difference in latitude between Çanakkale and the south coast, and hundreds of metres of difference in altitude between the coast and the mountains that soar vertically above them, all of which affects the climate. Generally, though, it is cool and damp in winter, almost perfect in spring and autumn, bakingly hot in summer, and icy cold with snow in the mountains in winter.

İzmir:	J	F	M	A	M	J	J	A	S	O	N	D
°C max	13	14	17	21	26	31	33	33	29	24	19	14
°C min	4	4	6	9	13	17	21	21	17	13	9	6
°F max	55	57	63	70	79	87	92	92	85	76	67	58
°F min	39	40	43	49	56	63	69	69	62	55	49	42

Antalya:	J	F	M	A	M	J	J	A	S	O	N	D
°C max	15	16	18	21	26	30	34	33	31	27	22	17
°C min	6	7	8	11	16	19	23	22	19	15	11	8
°F max	59	61	65	70	79	86	94	92	88	81	72	63
°F min	43	45	47	52	61	67	74	72	67	59	52	47

CLOTHING

Although the Turks are relatively laid-back and you do see plenty of Turkish women in the resorts wearing skimpy tops and short skirts, the country is overwhelmingly Muslim and it is good manners to leave beach wear on the beach and cover up when you go into town. Shorts are fine, but shouldn't be too short; miniskirts should be respectable and t-shirts should ideally cover both shoulders and navels. If visiting mosques, cover knees, shoulders and heads (women) and remove your shoes. When visiting archaeological sites or hiking in the mountains, you will need heavier duty walking shoes or boots for the rough paths. A hat and sunglasses are essentials in summer. In the evening men rarely need a jacket and tie – smart casual is the order of the day.

In winter, bring light pullovers and something waterproof; inland and in the north you may need full-blown winter gear.

CRIME AND SAFETY

The crime rate in Turkey is relatively low but you do need to watch out for pickpockets or purse-snatchers in crowded markets and bars. Most people are honest but some tradesmen consider it part of the game to get you to pay as much as possible (it's up to you to haggle). It is only when the occasional taxi driver takes you for an unnecessary drive halfway round Turkey or uses sleight of hand to confuse you over the change that things turn sour. If you always try to find out what the real price should be before you start negotiations and try to make sure you have plenty of small change, you are halfway towards solving the problems.

There are extremely harsh penalties for drugs (using or dealing) in Turkey, so steer well clear. The export of antiquities without a permit from the ministry is illegal. And remember that while the Turks tolerate alcohol, and many do drink, most Muslims do not. The sight of drunken tourists reeling round the streets, throwing up in the gutters, throwing punches at their fellow tourists and being carted off to hospital to have their stomachs pumped (all of which sadly happen all too frequently in some resorts) is not one to endear them to their hosts. On that point – remember that your fellow tourists are probably more likely than the Turks to commit crimes against you.

Women do not need to wear the veil but should dress sensibly and obey the same rules as anywhere else – don't walk around on your own at night, let someone know where you are going, use a bag with a zip and crossover strap, and don't go off with strangers. Carry a scarf with you in case you want to enter any of the more conservative mosques.

There is one additional, but remote, security risk in Turkey – occasional bomb attacks by both al Qaeda and the PKK, the Kurdish separatists. However, these are few and far between with target areas far from the tourist hotspots – you would have to be extraordinarily unlucky to be in the wrong place at the wrong time.

CUSTOMS AND ENTRY REQUIREMENTS

Citizens of Australia, Canada and New Zealand need only a valid passport to enter Turkey for stays of 90 days or less. Citizens of the US, Ireland and the UK require a valid passport and a visa, obtainable from Turkish consulates abroad or at the point of entry to Turkey. On entry, the fee is £10 for British subjects, €10 for Irish citizens and $20 for visitors from the US, which must be paid in hard currency; visas are considerably more expensive if obtained in advance. Visas are valid for multiple entries over 90 days, but cannot exceed the validity of your passport, and may not be issued if your passport is about to expire. In case of emergency, photocopy the identity page of your passport and the page on which your Turkish visa has been affixed and keep them separately from the passport. Contact the Turkish Consulate in London, tel: 020-7591 6900, or visit www.turkishconsulate.org.uk for further information.

Turkish regulations permit visitors to bring into the country duty free most personal effects, including 200 cigarettes, 50 cigars, and 200g of tobacco (you may buy an additional 400 cigarettes and 100 cigars at duty free on arrival), 1.5kg coffee, 1.5kg instant coffee, 500g of tea, 1kg of chocolate and 1kg of sweets and 5 litres of wine or spirits. Drugs and weapons are subject to heavy penalties, so if carrying drugs for medical reasons, bring a letter from your doctor. If you are carrying more than one camera, CD player, personal computer or video player, these items should be declared on arrival. Antiques leaving the country must be licensed; reputable dealers will obtain this licence for you.

Currency restrictions and VAT. You may import as much foreign currency as you like into Turkey, but there is a limit of US$5,500-worth of Turkish currency.

A value-added tax of 18 percent is added to most purchases in Turkey. Foreigners can claim a VAT refund on departure if they deal with qualified retailers (look for the certificate in the window) and are planning to leave the country within 90 days. Get a certificate from the retailer and present it with the receipt to the VAT refunds desk at the point of departure; you may be asked to produce the goods for inspection. Some retailers are prepared to refund the tax and deal with the paperwork themselves – don't be afraid to ask.

D

DRIVING

Drive on the right, pass on the left and give way to the right. The speed limit is 120km/h (70mph) on motorways, 90km/h (55mph) on rural roads, 50km/h (30mph) or 40km/h (25mp/h) in towns. Drivers and all passengers must wear seat belts, and motorcyclists must wear helmets. Look at signs carefully – parking is often highly restricted; many cities and towns have car parks at the fringes of commercial and tourist centres; use these whenever possible. There is a total ban on drink driving – even one beer or glass of wine will put you over the limit. There are regular police traps, particularly at the entrance to towns.

Durmak Yasaktır	No Stopping
Yol Yapımı	Men Working (Road Works)
Dikkat	Danger
Yavaş	Slow Down
Tek Yön	One-way
Giremez	No Entry
Şehir Merkezi	Town Centre

Some useful phrases:

Driver's licence	**Ehliyet**
Petrol	**Benzin**
Petrol station	**Benzin istasyonu**
Oil	**Motor yagi**
Tyre	**Lastik**
Brakes	**Frenler**
It does not work.	**Calismiyor.**
Fill the tank, please.	**Doldurum, lütfen.**
I've had a breakdown.	**Arabam arızalandı.**
There's been an accident.	**Bir kaza oldu.**

You may drive on your national driver's licence for up to three months, but as you should have a Turkish translation, it is probably best to get an international licence. If bringing a car into Turkey, you will need the log book, proof of ownership (or a power of attorney from the owner), a Green Card and carnet. Check you are comprehensively insured. An official nationality sticker must be displayed at the rear of the vehicle. Make sure your car is equipped with flares and a red warning triangle in case of breakdown, as well as a full set of spares.

Turkey's roads have been improving dramatically in recent years but you still need to take great care when driving here, with hazards including anything from herds of donkeys to wobbly old men carrying olive trees on the cross-bars of their bicycles, and the local Lewis Hamilton. Many of the coast roads twist along the cliffs with few proper barriers or markings, and signposting is quite often hidden behind a bush, a traffic light or round the corner. Traffic lights go straight from red to green and a flashing arrow means you can turn right if the road is clear even if the light is red.

In case of an accident or breakdown, dial the The Touring and Automobile Club of Turkey (TTOK) 24-hour emergency service (tel: 0212-280 4449, www.turing.org.tr). To call the traffic police dial 154. You must report all accidents to the police or your insurance may not cover you.

Petrol *(benzin)* and diesel *(mazot)* are readily available along all major roads. Petrol is available in super and normal grades, and lead-free *(kurşunsus)*. Fuel is hugely expensive by any standards; diesel is cheaper than petrol.

E

ELECTRICITY

220V/50Hz; continental-style two round-pin plugs.

EMBASSIES AND CONSULATES

Although all the embassies are in Ankara, countries also have consulates in Istanbul and there are also some in larger resorts.

Consulates (in Istanbul unless otherwise stated)
Australia: 2nd Floor, Suzer Plaza, Askerocagi Caddesi No. 15, tel: 0212-243 1333; Canada: Istiklal Caddesi 189/5, Beyoğlu, tel: 0212-251 9838; **Ireland:** Cumhuriyet Caddesi 26/A, Harbiye, tel: 0212-246 6025; **UK:** Mesrutiyet Caddesi 34, Tepebaşi/Beyoğlu, tel: 0212-334 6400; in Antalya: Gneclik Mah. 1314. Sk. 6/8, tel: 0242-244 5313; in Bodrum: Kibris Sehitlri Cad. Konacik Mevkii, 401/B, tel: 0252-319 0093; in İzmir: 1442 Sk. 49 Alsancak, tel: 0232-463 5151; and in Marmaris: Barbaros Caddesi 11, tel: 0252-412 6486; **US:** Kaplıcalar Mevkii 2, Istinye, tel: 0212-335 9000.

Embassies in Ankara
Australia: MNG Building, Ugur Mumcu Caddesi 88, 7th Floor, Gaziosmanpaşa, tel: 0312-459 9500; **Canada**: Cinnah Caddesi 58, Çankaya, tel: 0312-409 2700; **New Zealand**: 13/4 Iran Caddesi, Kavaklıdere, tel: 0312-467 9054; **UK:** Sehit Ersan Caddesi 46/A, Cankaya, tel: 0312-455 3344; **US:** Atatürk Bulv. 110, Kavaklıdere, tel: 0312-455 5555.

EMERGENCIES (see also POLICE)

Police 155 (you will be directed to specialised numbers if necessary)
Fire 110
Ambulance 112

Help!	**Imdat!**
I am ill.	**Hastayım.**
Call a doctor.	**Doktor cagirim.**
Where is the hospital?	**Nerede hastane?**

G

GAY AND LESBIAN TRAVELLERS

Turkish men frequently greet with a kiss and even walk hand in hand. This is not a sign of homosexuality. Homosexual activity between consenting adults over the age of 18 is legal and tolerated, but it is illegal to print and distribute material that promotes homosexuality and, on the whole, Turks do not accept homosexual lifestyles easily. Bodrum and Antalya in particular are relatively gay-friendly resorts, but overtly sexual behaviour between same sex couples should be avoided in public places.

GETTING THERE (see also AIRPORTS)

By air. The national carrier, Turkish Airlines (Central Reservations tel: 444 0849, www.thy.com), operates direct flights to İzmir and Antalya as well as numerous flights to all the coastal airports via Istanbul and Ankara. In addition, British Airways and other scheduled airlines fly into İzmir and Antalya, several low-cost airlines including easyJet (www.easyjet.com), Pegasus Air (www.flypgs.com), Onur (www.onurair.com.tr) and Atlas Jet (www.atlasjet.com) offer flights throughout the year and numerous charter airlines flock in between April and October. From the UK, the main charter operators include Thomas Cook, Avro, First Choice and Excel Airways.
By land. It is possible to get to Istanbul by train, but the journey is long (about 72 hours from London) and much more expensive than a flight, although it can become an adventure in its own right, with stops en route. This was the original route of the Orient Express, and the modern Orient Express (www.orient-express.com) still makes occasional visits to Istanbul. From there, trains leave from Haydarpaşa station on the Asian shore, for the rest of the country. The network is very limited and services are infrequent, but there are services to İzmir, Adana and Mersin.

Inter-Rail passes (for European travellers) are valid in Turkey, although the rail network is limited. For details contact Rail Europe (UK tel: 08448-484 064, www.raileurope.co.uk).

It will take at least four days to drive to Turkey from most places in Western Europe. The most expedient route is to drive to Italy and continue from there to Turkey by ferry.

There are lots of cheap long-distance coaches networking all over Turkey, connecting every town and city. Every route is served by several companies but there is no single website or even a single ticket office at the bus station. To get around the chaotic tangle of prices and timetabling, use the local travel agents for your bookings. The buses leave from the main bus station *(otogar)* in each town.

By sea. There are ferries between Brindisi and Ancona in Italy and Çeşme from April to November with Marmara Lines (tel: 0232-712 2223, www.marmaralines.com); from Turkish Cyprus to several south-coast cities including Alanya (tel: 0242-511 5358, www. fergun.net); and links to Bodrum and Marmaris from Rhodes and Kos, while other towns have services and sightseeing tours to nearby Greek islands. Deniz Lines (tel: 0212-444 3369, www.denizline.com.tr) runs a car ferry between Istanbul and Bodrum in July–September.

GUIDES AND TOURS

There are thousands of tours and guides on offer, from full-blown package tours, to day trips sold by travel agents and operators in the resorts, to state-licensed guides and small boys hanging around sights hoping for a tip.

H

HEALTH AND MEDICAL CARE

You don't need any inoculations for travel to Turkey and there are no serious health risks, although the coastal area east of Alanya does have malaria in season. The most common problems for tourists are mild stomach upsets, sunburn and/or heat stroke in high summer, and alcohol poisoning. All are easily avoided – keep washing your hands, drink bottled water, eat only freshly cooked, hygienically prepared food; wear a hat and sunblock and drink plenty of water; and keep the alcohol levels down. Also, be careful in the countryside – there are poisonous scorpions, snakes and spiders.

Make sure you have full travel insurance that will cover any medical treatment you may need. You may be asked to pay for treatment upfront, so keep all receipts. Pharmacies are well stocked, and can treat many minor ailments; emergency after-hour locations are posted in all pharmacies. Your hotel will be able to get you a doctor if necessary. The quality of medical care is generally good.

Where can I find a doctor/ dentist?	**Nereden bir doktor/ bir disci bulabilirim?**
Where is the nearest pharmacy?	**En yakin eczane nerededir?**
Sunburn	**Güneş yanğı**
Fever	**Ateş**
Stomach ache	**Mide bozulması**

HOLIDAYS

1 January	New Year's Day
23 April	National Independence and Children's Day
19 May	Atatürk Commemoration and Youth and Sports Day
30 August	Victory Day
29 October	Republic Day (anniversary of the declaration of the Turkish Republic)
10 November	Anniversary of Atatürk's death

Important Muslim holidays, such as Kurban Bayramı (Feast of the Sacrifice of Abraham) and Şeker Bayramı (the 3-day Sugar Festival celebrating the end of the month-long Ramazan fast) are also celebrated, moving through the year according to the lunar calendar.

L

LANGUAGE

English is widely spoken in the resorts but it is greatly appreciated if you have a few words of Turkish. The language uses the Roman alphabet and pronunciation is very literal as long as you know what to do with the accents:

c like j in jam
ç like ch in chip
ğ almost silent, lengthening the preceding vowel
h always pronounced
ı like i in sir
j like s in pleasure
ö like ur in fur
ş like sh in shell
ü like ew in few

Some basic words and phrases:

Good morning	**Günaydın**	Goon-eye-DEN
Please	**Lütfen**	LEWT-fen
Thank you	**Teşekkür ederim**	Tay-shake-kur eh-day-REEM
Bon appetit	**Afiyet olsun**	
Cheers!	**Şerefe!**	
Excuse me	**Ozur dilerim**	Oh-ZEWR deel-air-eem
Where is...?	**Nerde...?**	NEH-deer...?
I don't understand	**Anlamıyorum**	Ahn-LAH-muh-yohr-um
I'd like...	**Istiyorum...**	EES-tee-yohr-ruhm
How much is that?	**Bu ne kadar?**	boo neh kaddar?
Tuvalet var mı?	**Is there a toilet here?**	
OK	**Tamam**	
Yes/No	**Evet/Hayır**	

Numbers:

one	**bir**	beer
two	**iki**	ee-KEE
three	**üc**	ooch
four	**dört**	doort
five	**beş**	besh
six	**altı**	ahl-TUH
seven	**yedi**	YED-dee
eight	**sekiz**	sek-KEEZ
nine	**dokuz**	doh-KOOZ
ten	**on**	ohn
hundred	**yüz**	yewz

Days of the week:

Monday	**Pazartesi**	Pahz-AHR-teh-see
Tuesday	**Salı**	SAHL-luh
Wednesday	**Çarşamba**	Char-shahm-BAH
Thursday	**Perşembe**	Pair-shem-BAH
Friday	**Cuma**	JOON-ahz
Saturday	**Cumartesi**	Joom-AHR-teh-see
Sunday	**Pazar**	Pahz-AHR

M

MAPS

Navigating along the coast is fairly simple, with one main road (and off-shoots) that follows the coast the whole way. There are plenty of maps on sale locally, most slightly out of date, but no more out of date than those you will buy elsewhere. Town plans are usually only available from the tourist offices, although you first have to find the tourist office without the help of a map.

MEDIA

Some foreign newspapers are usually available at newsstands in the larger resorts, and there is an English-language paper, the *Turkish Daily News*, widely available in cities and resorts, which also have a selection of English and German magazines and websites with what's on listings, restaurant reviews and properties for sale. The government-run Tourism Radio broadcasts news and other programming in English, 8.30–10.30am and 12.30–6.30pm daily. You will find it on FM bands throughout the country, usually between 100 and 102 MHz. Most hotels have satellite TV, with *BBC World*, *CNN* and other English-language stations.

MONEY

The Yeni Türk Lira (YTL, new Turkish Lira; plural yetiler) is broken into 100 kuruş, which are available in 1, 5, 10, 20 and 50 kuruş coins. There are also 1 and 2 YTL coins and 1, 5, 10, 20, 50 and 100 YTL notes.

Banks usually open Mon–Fri 8.30am–noon and 1.30–5pm, with a few in major resorts opening on Saturday morning. At least one bank in each town will have a currency exchange, but by far the easiest way to get cash these days is to use the ubiquitous ATM machines. Credit cards are usable in most places, but may attract a small percentage premium in some shops. Most shopkeepers happily trade in lira, US dollars, euros or GB pounds.

OPENING HOURS

Times can vary hugely, but as a rough guide opening hours are as follows: archaeological sites, 8am–6pm daily; banks, 8.30am–noon and 1.30–5pm, Mon–Fri; government offices, 8.30am–12.30pm and 1.30–5.30pm, Mon–Fri (tourist offices are often open at weekends as well in summer); museums, 9.30am–12.30pm, 1.30–5.30pm Tue–Sun; post offices, 8.30am–12.30pm and 1.30–5.30pm; restaurants, noon–2.30 or 3pm for lunch, 7 or 7.30pm–10 or 10.30pm for dinner (those that have music and offer drinks will sometimes remain open into the small hours); shops, 9.30am–7pm (as late as midnight during the summer season in some resorts).

P

POLICE *(polis)*

Turkey has several different types of police. The *Polis* deal with day-to-day petty crime, traffic, and parking; the national *Jandarma*, actually a branch of the army, handles serious crime and civilian unrest, and government protection; the *Trafik Polis* take over traffic duties in large towns and cities; the market police, *Belediye Zabitası*, deal with traders and shoppers in the markets; and the *Turizm Polis*, who often speak English, should be your first port of call in the resorts. To call the police, dial 155.

Where's the nearest police station?   **En yakim karakol nerede?**

POST OFFICES

Look for the PTT sign to find the post office. The central post office in major cities will stay open from 8am–midnight; the rest open 8.30am–12.30pm and 1.30–5.30pm. In addition to postal services they offer telephone and fax services and some provide currency exchange. The postal service is reliable but slow. Express service is faster but much more expensive and most people resort to courier companies such as Fedex or DHL when sending anything valuable or urgent.

PUBLIC TRANSPORT

It is perfectly possible to have a holiday in Turkey without your own transport, using a combination of tours and taxis, buses, and dolmuş (shared taxis that run along set routes between the local villages). If using public transport to visit archaeological sites, make sure you have organised a way to get back to your hotel as well. Wherever you are going, take the address with you in written form for when your appalling Turkish accent gets the better of you (make sure you have the phone number as well, in case you need to get directions) and, if possible, get a map; local taxi drivers rarely know their way around well. And check what the fare should be before setting out, check that the meter is on or, if the taxi driver insists on a fixed fare, haggle.

When is the next bus to...?	**Bir sonraki otobüs kaçta kalkiyor...?**
A ticket to...	**a bir bilet...**
What time does it leave?	**Kaçta kalkiyor?**
How long does it take?	**Ne kadar surebilir?**
How much does it cost?	**Ne kadar?**

R

RELIGION

Religion in Turkey is a little complicated at the moment. Turkey is a secular state and proud to be so, but 99 percent of its inhabitants are Muslims – and proud to be so. Most are relatively moderate, but the government is currently led by the religious AK Party and it is fashionable to be more religious. Some 62 percent of Turkish women now wear the veil and numbers are growing.

As non-Muslims you will not be expected to cover up, although women should dress with a little decorum away from the beach, and it is fine to drink alcohol (although getting drunk is socially unacceptable). You may enter mosques, but should remove your shoes, cover shoulders, knees and (if female) heads.

T

TELEPHONE

The Turkish mobile phone network, based on the European standard GSM operating system, is excellent.

There are relatively few public call boxes, but they do still exist, taking credit cards or phone cards, which can be bought in post offices and newsstands.

Local calls are very inexpensive, but international roaming is hugely expensive and most hotels apply large surcharges to long-distance calls. For cheaper calls, either buy a local pay-as-you-go sim card or an international roaming sim card (www.sim4travel. co.uk or www.gosim.co.uk). Prepaid international phone cards, sold at newsstands, can be used with hotel phones, although some hotels still charge a premium.

To call internationally, first dial 00, then the country code (1 for the US and Canada, 44 for the UK, 353 for the Republic of Ireland, 61 for Australia, 64 for New Zealand, 27 for South Africa). For directory assistance, dial 118.

TIME ZONES

GMT +2 in winter, with daylight saving time taking it to GMT +3 between April and October. This puts Turkey 2 hours ahead of London, 7 hours ahead of New York, 10 hours ahead of Los Angeles, 9 hours behind Sydney, and 11 hours behind Auckland.

New York	London	**Turkey**	Sydney	Los Angeles
5am	10am	**noon**	9pm	2am

TIPPING

There is usually a service charge included on restaurant bills, but it is customary to leave a few coins as well for good service; if there is no service charge, tip 10–15 percent. Tip porters about 1YTL a bag, and leave about 2YTL per day of your stay for a hotel chambermaid. In many small hotels the staff double up as cleaners, receptionists, waiters and concierge, so leave a generous tip on departure. It is not customary to tip taxi drivers, although you can simply round up the total. Tour guides, excursion-boat operators, and other tourist providers also expect a tip; allow 5–10YTL per person per day as a yardstick for good service.

TOILETS *(tuvalet)*

There are plenty of public toilets these days, with most cafés and restaurants, garages and tourists sights having facilities. Most are clean and tidy although some are still squat style (some offer a choice, so look in all the cubicles). Some come with a guard and a price tag of up to 1YTL; even so, it is probably worth carrying your own stash of tissues as toilet paper is something of a rarity; in some places you will be asked to put the paper in a basket next to the toilet and not flush it. Gents are marked '*bay*' and ladies '*bayan*'.

TOURIST INFORMATION

The official Turkish tourism websites are www.goturkey.com, www.tourismturkey.org and www.gototurkey.co.uk. Turkish Tourist Offices abroad:

UK: 4th Floor, 29–30 St James' Street, London SW1A 1HB, tel: 020-7839 7778/4, email: info@gototurkey.co.uk.

US: 821 United Nations Plaza, New York, NY 10017, tel: 212-687 2194, email: ny@tourismturkey.org; 2525 Massachusetts Avenue, Washington, DC, tel: 202-612 6800, email: dc@tourismturkey.org; 5055 Wilshire Boulevard, Los Angeles, CA 90036, tel: 323-937 8066, email: la@tourismturkey.org.

Tourist offices in Turkey
Antalya: Cumhuriyet Caddesi, Ozel Idare Alti 2, tel: 0242-241 1747; **Ayvalık:** Yat Limanı Çarşısı, tel: 0266-312 2122; **Bergama:** Bergama Hükümet Konaği, B Blok Zemin Kat, tel: 0232-6312851; **Bodrum:** Bariş Meydanı 48, tel: 0252-316 1091; **Çannakale:** (provincial Directorate) Kayserili Ahmet Paşa Caddesi, tel: 0286-217-2371; **Çeşme:** İskele Meydanı 8, tel: 0232-712 6653; **Dalaman:** Airport, tel: 0252-792 5220; **Fethiye:** Karagözler Mah., Fevzi Çakmak Caddesi, İskele Mey. 1/A, tel: 0252-614 1527; **İzmir:** Akdeniz Mah., 1344 Sokak 2, Pasaport, tel: 0232-445 7390; **Kaş:** Cumhuriyet Meydanı 5, tel: 0242-836 1238; **Kuşadası:** Liman Caddesi 13, tel: 0256-614 1103; **Marmaris:** İskele Meydanı 2, tel: 0252-412 1035; **Pamukkale:** Örenyeri Pamukkale, tel: 0258-272 2077; **Selçuk:** Atatürk Mah., Agora Çarşısı 35, tel: 0232-892 6328.

WEBSITES

www.goturkey.com
www.tourismturkey.org
www.gototurkey.co.uk
www.antalya.ws.com
www.bodrumlife.com
www.enjoykalkan.com
www.marmaris4u.com
www.walkizmir.com

YOUTH HOSTELS

There are very few youth hostels and those that exist are of poor quality, but there are plenty of good small pensions and B&Bs, which make up for the shortfall.

Recommended Hotels

The Turkish Coast has huge numbers of hotels, of every shape, size, and price, from giant all-inclusive holiday villages to chic boutique hotels, tiny *pansiyons* and, increasingly, self-catering villas and apartments (*see also A–Z, page 107*). With limited space, we include only those that we can whole-heartedly recommend – they must have great character, be well located, provide excellent value, be particularly friendly or be unusually well equipped with amenities. We welcome your comments and suggestions for future editions. Reservations are essential in better hotels almost anywhere in high season, and are highly recommended at other times.

The symbols below indicate the price range for a double room with bath, including breakfast, in high season; they will be considerably lower at other times, although many coastal hotels close between November and April.

$$$$$	above £200
$$$$	£130–200
$$$	£75–130
$$	£50–75
$	below £50

AEGEAN COAST

AYVACIK

Berceste Hotel $$$ *Sivrice Feneri MV, Bektas Köyü, 17860, Ayvacık, tel: 0286-723 4616, www.bercestehotel.com.* Rustic stone walls, flagged floors and wooden beams are the order of the day at this hillside guesthouse with fabulous views over the village of Sivrice, near Assos, to the sea. There is a pebble beach 400m downhill.

AYVALIK

Kelebek Pension $ *Mareşal Çakmak Caddesi 108, tel: 0266-312 3908, www.kelebek-pension.com.* A simple, attractive Turkish-

Dutch run pension in the town centre, with a terrace, bikes, a telescope and library and two guest kitchens along with five bedrooms. Three minutes' walk to the sea.

BEHRAMKALE

Assos Kervansaray $$ *Behramkale, Ayvacık 17860, tel: 0286-721 7093, fax: 0286-721 7200, www.assoskervansaray.com.* One of the larger hotels in this lovely little resort, this 43-room boutique hotel in an old stone house offers indoor and outdoor pools, a choice of restaurants, one a seaside terrace beside the fishing harbour.

Biber Evi $$ *village centre, tel: 0286-721 7410, www.biberevi.com.* Tiny restored Ottoman house with beautifully restored rooms (wood panelled walls and antique furnishings), and an excellent restaurant in the courtyard, serving fusion food with home-made jams and chutneys. No single night bookings.

ÇANAKKALE

Anzac Hotel $$$ *Saat Kulesi Meydanı 8, tel: 0286-217 7777, fax: 0286-217 2906, www.anzachotel.com.* Themed around the local sights, including Gallipoli and Troy, this boutique hotel is a popular base with comfortable rooms, two restaurants and a rooftop bar. They also organise some of the best tours of the Gallipoli peninsula.

Kolin Hotel $$$$ *Kepez, tel: 0286-218 0808, fax: 0286-218 0800, www.kolinhotel.com.* Located just outside the centre, overlooking the Dardanelles, this boxy white and mirror-glass resort has 276 rooms, a private beach, indoor and outdoor pools, sports facilities, a selection of restaurants, bars and entertainment.

ÇEŞME

Sheraton Çeşme $$$$ *Sifme Caddesi 35, Ilıca, tel: 0232-723 1240, www.sheratoncesme.com.* They don't necessarily adapt to their environment, but this Sheraton, like others, is an oasis of sumptuous luxury, with a private beach and one of the best spas in the area.

Alaçat Kirevi $$$ *3012 s. no. 2 Yenimecidiye m. Alaçati 35950,* *tel: 0232-716 6961, fax: 0232-716 8816, www.alacat.com.tr.* A pretty little 8-room pension, run by the owners of a local art and antiques shop, with stone walls, a lovely terrace and garden and laid-back house-party atmosphere.

İZMIR

Beyond Boutique Hotel $$$$ *1376 Caddesi 5, Alsançak, İzmir,* *tel: 0232-463 0585, fax: 0232-463 0586, www.hotelbeyond.com.* A trendy new city centre hotel, stylishly designed using coloured light (for Chakra therapy), with a restaurant, bar, massage, sauna and parking. 60 rooms and suites.

Crown Plaza İzmir $$$ *Inciraltı Caddesi 67, 35340 Balçova, İzmir,* *tel: 0232-292 1300, fax: 0232-292 1313, http://cpizmir.com.* One of the newest and best of the crop of İzmir's new hotels, a round mirrored tower in a quiet seafront location with all the facilities and a regular shuttle into the city centre.

KUŞADASI

Anzac Golden Bed Boutique Pension $ *Arslanlar Caddesi Ugurlu 1, Cikmazi 4, tel: 0256-614 8708, fax: 0256-614 8708.* Friendly Turkish-Australian run pension 10 minutes' walk away from the city centre and the beach, with great views from terrace bar, grill and most rooms.

Club Caravanserail $$ *Atatürk Bulv. 2, 09400 Kuşadası, tel: 0256-614 4115, fax: 0256-614 2423, www.kusadasihotels.com/caravan serail.* A 17th-century caravanserai, carefully restored, furnished with antiques and kilims. Restaurant and club, with folk music and belly dancing. Great fun, if noisy at times. 26 rooms and 1 suite.

PAMUKKALE

Venus Hotel $ *Pamuk Mh. Hasan Tahsin Cd, No 16 Pamukkale,* *tel: 0258-272 2152, fax: 0258-272 2993, www.venushotel.net.* A friendly family-run pension in Pamukkale village attractively furnished with kilims, carpets and traditional furniture, and with a small garden and pool. The restaurant has a good selection of vegetarian food as well as the usual offerings.

SELÇUK

Kale Han $ *İzmir Cad. 49, 35920 Selçuk, tel: 0232-892 6154, fax: 0232-892 2169, www.kalehan.com.* With lovely gardens, a great setting, a pool, delicious food, plenty of family memorabilia and antiques and a warm and friendly welcome, this small hotel, built in traditional style at the foot of the castle, has become a firm local favourite. 58 rooms.

TURQUOISE COAST

BODRUM

Aegean Gate Hotel $$ *Akçabük Mevki, Kumbahçe Mh., Güvercin Sok, No. 2, Bodrum, tel: 0252-316 7853, fax: 0252-313 4973, www.aegeangatehotel.com.* Beautiful little Irish-owned hotel (2–4-person apartments and 4 suites) in a dramatically rocky cove about 10 minutes from the centre from Bodrum, with an excellent pool, bar and restaurant.

Kempinski Hotel Barbaros Bay $$$$ *Kizilagac Koyu Gerenkuyu Mevkii, 48400 Bodrum, tel: 0252-311 0303, www.kempinski-bodrum.com.* A gorgeous resort with all the frills including a sumptuous Six Senses spa, several excellent restaurants and a private beach, all set on a virtually private bay about 15 minutes drive from the town centre. 173 rooms and suites.

Lavanta Hotel $$$ *Yalikavak-Bodrum, 48430, tel: 0252-385 2167, fax: 0252-385 2290, www.lavanta.com.* A friendly Turkish-German boutique hotel overlooking the marina and rocky hillside of a small village 16km (10 miles) from Bodrum. 8 rooms and 12 apartments are spacious and airy, with terraces, a large pool and fabulous views, while the restaurant serves wonderful home-cooked food.

Majesty Hotel Marina Vista $$$ *Neyzen Tevfik Caddesi 222, tel: 0252-316 2260, fax: 0252-316 2347, www.majesty.com.tr.* An attractive four-star hotel opposite the marina in the town centre with a courtyard pool, restaurant, bar/coffee shop, and massage. It can be a little noisy, but is very convenient if you want to party. 85 rooms.

DALYAN

Dalyan Resort $$$ *Maraş Mah., Kaunos Sok. 50, tel: 0252-284 5499, fax: 0252-284 5498, www.dalyanresort.com. UK bookings via Anatolian Sky Holidays, tel: 0845-365 1011 or 0121-764 3550, www.anatoliansky.co.uk.* Charming little low-rise hotel hidden behind the reeds on the riverbank with courtyard pool, small spa (including mud treatments), excellent food and lovely views of the rock tombs.

MARMARIS

Dionysos Hotel $$$ *Alic Mevkii, Kumlubuk, tel: 0252-476 7957/ 7556, UK bookings via Exclusive Escapes, tel: +44-020-8605 3500, www.exclusiveescapes.co.uk.* Gorgeous hideaway boutique hotel in the mountains on the Bozburun peninsula near Turunc, with fabulous views, generous rooms, two restaurants, infinity pool, spa and a 5-minute drive down the mountain to the hotel's private beach.

Maritim Hotel Grand Azur $$$$ *Kenan-Eren Bulv. 13, 48700 Marmaris, tel: 0252-417 4050, fax: 0252-417 4060, www.hotel grandazur.com.* As sleek as a cruise ship moored on a private beach 2km (1 mile) from Marmaris town centre, this is the best of the 5-star resorts in town, with several pools, kids' clubs, and watersports of all sorts. 288 rooms and suites.

MEDITERRANEAN COAST

ALANYA

Kaptan $ *İskele Caddesi 70, tel: 0242-513 4900, fax: 0242-513 2000, www.kaptanhotels.com.* A well-established 49-room hotel near the Red Tower in the town centre, this is a far cry from the giant resorts that line Incekum beach, but it is a great (and very affordable) base for those who want to explore. Pool, terrace, bar and restaurant. The same group runs the much larger and flashier Grand Kaptan.

ANTALYA

Alp Paşa Hotel $$$ *Barbaros Mahallesi, Hesapçı Sokak 30–32, Kaleiçi, tel: 0242-247 5676, fax: 0242-248 5074, www.alppasa. com.* Built as a traditional caravanserai surrounding several original Ottoman buildings, this 60-room boutique hotel is probably the most upmarket within the walls of the old city, with antique-filled rooms, a pool, garden bar and excellent courtyard restaurant.

Hillside Su $$$$ *Konyaalti, tel: 0242-249 0700, fax: 0242-249 0707, www.hillsidesu.com.* Antalya's funkiest hotel, a blindingly cool sea of white, from the floors upwards – accented in red, with live goldfish and great seas of mirrors. With a sumptuous spa, private beach, fine dining and dancing, and very close to the city.

Hotel Minyon $$$ *Kılınçaslan Mah. Tabakhane Sok. 31, Kaleiçi, Antalya, tel: 0242-247 1147, www.minyonhotel.com.* A small but very carefully restored Ottoman house with understated elegance and friendly staff, in the backstreets of the old town, with a small courtyard garden and plunge pool. Bed and breakfast and snacks.

Villa Perla $$ *Barbaros Mahallesi, Hesapçı Sokak 26, Kaleiçi, tel: 0242-248 9793, fax: 0242-241 2917, www.villaperla.com.* Beautifully restored little family-run Ottoman house hotel with a garden, pool and excellent restaurant serving some of the best vegetarian food in town. 10 rooms.

BELEK

Ela Quality Resort $$$$ *İskele Mevkii, Belek, tel: 0242-710 2200, www.elaresort.com.* Very gilded, glamorous and cosmopolitan, this is one of the newest of the many 5-star resorts catering to golfers, with a private beach, plenty of other sports facilities and evening entertainment on tap to keep them entertained between rounds.

LykiaWorld and Links Golf Antalya $$$ *Denizyaka Köyü, Köprüçay Mevkii, PK: 31 07600 Antalya, tel: 0242-754 4343, fax: 0242-754 4344, www.lykiaworldantalya.com.* Sleek, low-rise hotel set between the dunes of Turkey's only seaside golf courses, halfway between Belek and Side. As well as golf there's a spa, shopping, a kids' club, great food, watersports, several pools and plenty of other entertainment on offer.

FETHIYE

Hillside Beach Club $$$$ *Kalemya Koyu, tel: 0252-614 8360, fax: 0252-614 1470, www.hillside.com.tr.* A holiday village set in a remote private bay with everything on offer from watersports to dance parties that light up the surrounding hills with laser displays, signature restaurants, kids' clubs, a nature spa, plus boat trips and sightseeing excursions.

Villa Daffodil $$ *Fevzi Çakmak Cad. 115, Karagözler, tel: 0252-614 9595, fax: 0252-612 2223, www.villadaffodil.com.* On the waterfront about 1km from the town centre, this pretty 27-room hotel was built in the traditional Ottoman style. The rooms have balconies, there is a pool, a sauna and a restaurant. Early booking advised.

KALKAN

Lizo Hotel $ *Milli Egemenlik Caddesi, Kalamar Yolu 57, Pk 110 Kalkan, tel: 0242-844 3381, http://lizohotel.com.* Small, family-run hotel at the back of the town, with restaurant, bar, garden and pool. Great views, friendly service and excellent food make this a firm favourite, in spite of the steep walk back after dinner or the beach.

Kalkan Regency Hotel $$$ *Cumhuriyet Caddesi, Gonca Sok 2/6, Kalkan, tel: 0242-844 2230, fax: 0242-844 3290, UK bookings via Exclusive Escapes, tel: 020-8605 3500, www.exclusiveescapes.co.uk.* Cosy boutique hotel on the edge of the village with a friendly house-party atmosphere, fabulous views, every luxury including its own gulet, yacht and wellness centre. The Seapoint Terrace restaurant is one of the best in town.

KAŞ

Deniz Feneri Lighthouse $$$$ *Metin Toker Sokak, Beyan Cenkci Cadessi Cukurbag Yarimadasi Kaş 07580, tel: 0242-836 2741, UK bookings via Exclusive Escapes, tel: 020-8605 3500, www.exclusive escapes.co.uk.* Chic little hotel on the Kaş peninsula, with modern design, huge picture windows over superb views, and fabulous food.

Gardenia Otel $$ *Hükümet Cad. 47, Küçükçakıl, 07580 Kafl, tel: 0242-836 2368, fax: 0242-836 2891, www.gardeniahotel-kas.com.* Small hotel with a personal touch. No bar or pool, but you can swim at the club across the road and there are plenty of bars nearby; meals are served on the terrace. 12 rooms. Open Apr–mid-Nov.

ÖLÜDENIZ

Hotel Montana Pine Resort $$$$ *Ovacık Mahallesi, Ölüdeniz Beldesi, tel: 0252-616 7108, fax: 0252-616 6451, www.montana pine.com.* Set in the pine forests overlooking the lagoon, this pretty timber-framed hotel has pools for those who don't want to take the shuttle down to the beach. 150 rooms, several restaurants, bars and cafés, tennis court, fitness centre and massage.

Lykia World $$$ *PK 102, Ölüdeniz, tel: 0252-617 0300, fax: 0252-617 0350, www.lykiagroup.com.* Huge holiday village in a private bay about 3km (2 miles) from Ölüdeniz. Choose to stay in the spread out Village or smaller Residence. Kids' club, adults-only pool, nudist beach and spa, plus paragliding, waterskiing and diving all available. Several buffet-style restaurants.

PHASELIS

Sundance Nature Village $–$$ *Tekirova, tel: 0242-821 4165, fax: 0242-821 5527, www.sundancecamp.com.* Clean and simple accommodation (en suite) in cabins with a fan, or bring your own tent. The food is plain, good and plentiful, the company interesting, the landscape lovely with plenty of wild flowers and wildlife, beach, walking, horses for riding and activities from yoga to painting.

Recommended Restaurants

Turkey claims to be the home of one of the world's four great cuisines (along with France, Italy and China). Those who don't stray beyond the lamb kebab might not experience the full glory that the country has to offer, but search out the better restaurants and you are in for a treat. We have chosen a range of restaurants to try and cover all options and price brackets, whether you want a quick snack or a gourmet feast – but there are plenty more to choose from. Many of the hotels listed previously have excellent restaurants.

Unless indicated otherwise, these restaurants are open daily for lunch and dinner; some open all day, serving breakfast and staying open until the last person staggers out at dawn. As a basic guide to what you can expect to pay, we have used the following symbols to give an indication of the price of a full meal for one, excluding alcohol.

$$$$	over £25
$$$	£15–25
$$	£10–15
$	below £10

AEGEAN COAST

AYVALIK

Canli Balik $$–$$$ *On Ayvalık Pier, south of Atatürk Bulvarı, tel: 0266-313 0081*. One of the most romantic settings imaginable, next to the fishing harbour, beside the sea, with the moon above; crisp white linen and candlelight, and wonderful seafood from simple grills to calamaris and baby anchovies in olive oil.

BERGAMA

Ticaret Odası Lokali $$ *Ulucamii Mahalesi, Büyükalan mevkii, tel: 0232-632 9641*. An old Greek building with a shady terrace and garden with views across the basilica and acropolis, with a good range of *meze*, kebabs and steaks.

ÇANAKKALE

Doyum Pide ve Kebap Restaurant $ *Cumhuriyet Meydanı 13, tel: 0286-217 4810*. People queue for the simple but utterly delicious pide and kebabs at this basic restaurant near the ferry port. No alcohol, takeaway available.

Yalova $$$ *Gümrük Sok, Liman Cad., tel: 0286-217 1045*. There are many fish restaurants along the Çanakkale seafront, but this one, near the ferry port, is undoubtedly the best, with wonderfully imaginative food including seafood *mezes* and fine views across the Dardanelles from the rooftop terrace. Open all year.

ÇEŞME

Sevim Café $$ *Hal Binası 5, opposite Kervansaray, tel: 0232-712 9647*. A slightly noisy but friendly local café in the main square by the sea, specialising in *mantı* (ravioli) and grilled meats.

GALLIPOLI PENINSULA

Gelibolu Liman Lokantası $$ *İç Limanı 20, Gelibolu, tel: 0286-566 1125*. A very friendly neighbourhood restaurant on the harbour front in Gelibolu, serving ultra-fresh fish at reasonable prices, including some interesting variations such as seafood salads and dolma.

Liman Restaurant *İsmet Paşa Mah. İstiklal Caddesi 67, Eceabat, tel: 0286-814 2755*. The normal Turkish mix of fish, meat and *meze*, all freshly prepared in simple surroundings with a sea view – a great lunch stop during a tour of the peninsula, that has been a firm local favourite for decades.

İZMIR

Asansör Ceneviz Meyhanesi $$$ *Mithatpaşa Cad. Dario Moreno Sok, İzmir, tel: 0232-255 5420*. Take the lift up to the top of the city and just near the exit is this hugely popular restaurant, with fantastic views across the city and bay to go with the delicious seafood.

Deniz $$$ *Atatürk Cad. 188 (in İzmir Palas Hotel), tel: 0232-422 0601.* Seafood is the speciality here with some wonderful options from jumbo prawns to swordfish kebabs, but there is also a mouth-watering array of *meze*. Outdoor terrace in summer.

Ristorante Pizzeria Venedik $$ *1382 Gül Sokak 10B, Alsancak, tel: 0232-422 2735.* Generally reckoned to serve the best pizzas in town, but also a good range of other options, including pasta, steak, chicken and desserts.

KUŞADASI

Ali Baba $$$ *Belediye Turistik Carşısı 5, tel: 0256-614 1551.* The sea view is great, but the heaped display of seafood at the entrance is far more spectacular, promising an imaginative collection of *meze*.

Ferah Balık $$ *İskele Yanı Güvercin Parkı İçi, tel: 0256-614 1281.* It isn't chic but this friendly fish restaurant right next to the fishing harbour has an outdoor terrace and delicious, simple fresh fish.

SELÇUK

Artemis *Şirince, tel: 0232-898 3201.* A fabulous setting overlooking this beautiful old Greek village, with delicious *meze*, grills and baked lamb, washed down with lashings of locally produced wine.

TURQUOISE COAST

BODRUM

Berk Balık $$$ *Cumhuriyet Caddesi 167, tel: 0252-313 0239.* Open daily noon–midnight. It can get noisy with the local bars in full swing, but this two-storey town centre fish restaurant offers an outdoor terrace, seaview and excellent seafood. Meat dishes also available.

Kırçiçeği $$ *Atatürk Bulvari 252, tel: 0252-319 0555.* Open 24 hours. The local branch of a chain serving excellent pizza and pide, grills and kebabs at reasonable prices.

Mimoza $$$$ *Yalı Mevkii 44/1, Gümüşlük, tel: 0252-394 3139.* Probably the best seafood restaurant on the Bodrum peninsula, in a delightful setting on the waterfront and with a perfect view of the sunset.

Sünger Pizza $ *Neyzen Tevfik Caddesi 216, Bodrum, tel: 0252-316 0854.* Open all day every day. The oldest restaurant in Bodrum, this popular hangout offers everything from pizzas and salad to seafood and schnitzel, and a garden to relax in.

DALYAN

Denizatı $$ *Çarşı İçi, tel: 0252-284 2129.* Not the most glamorous of the riverside restaurants, but right in the town centre, with waterside tables overlooking the dramatically lit rock tombs. Serves good traditional food alongside the pizzas and steaks, and very fresh fish.

Sini $$ *Yalı Caddesi, tel: 0252-284 5033.* Drift back into history and spend an evening the Ottoman way, lounging on cushions round a low table, eating traditional kebabs cooked in a clay pot.

MARMARIS

Bedesten Café and Bar $ *Çeşme Meydanı, tel: 0252-412 8838.* A 12th-century caravanserai in the bazaar, lovingly restored with comfy sofas to make a lovely shady place to while away the heat of the day.

Pineapple $$$ *Nestel Marina, tel: 0252-412 0976.* Excellent international cuisine (with an emphasis on Italian) surrounded by the gently waving masts of the international yachting brigade – live the good life on Marmaris seafront.

Istanbul Restaurant $ *Kemer Alti Cad. 4, tel: 0252-413 4523.* A tiny restaurant in the upstairs room of a private home in a side alley near the castle – simple well-cooked food and a limited menu. Cash only.

ALANYA

Mahperi Restaurant $$ *Rıhtım Caddesi, tel: 0242-512 5491.* Long-standing harbour front favourite (since 1947) serving an eclectic mix of everything from breakfast omelettes to fish casseroles and fillet steak, with a good selection of vegetarian food as well.

Red Tower Brewery *Iskele Caddesi 80, Alanya, tel: 0242-513 6664.* A harbour front tower of entertainment, with six floors, near the Red Tower – with a microbrewery, sports bar and sky lounge, classical Turkish, seafood and international restaurants. Take your pick.

ANTALYA

Antalya Balık Evi $$$$ *Çağlayan Mah. 2061 Sok. 1, Eski Lara Yolu, tel: 0242-323 1823.* Seafood, a sea view, a superb selection of *meze*, a garden, a swimming pool and 300 of the trendiest people on the south coast around you at this chic city restaurant.

Kral Sofrası $$$ *Yacht Harbour, tel: 0242-241 2198.* A restored Ottoman house in the old harbour with a garden and antique-furnished dining room, this well-respected and long-standing local favourite specialises in seafood, although there are other options available.

Yedi (7) Mehmet $$$ *Atatürk Kültür Parkı İçi, tel: 0242-238 5200.* Although it moved here only a few years ago, this legendary Antalya restaurant first opened in 1948 as a soup kitchen. It is more upmarket these days, with a range of perfectly presented fish and meat dishes.

AKSU

Anadolu Park $$ *Serik Caddesi, Konak Mh. Aksu Çıkısı, Aksu, tel: 0242-426 2400.* A destination restaurant hugely popular with the Antalya middle classes who pour out here for Sunday brunch. Choose between brunch, à la carte meals, or barbecue packs. Also children's playgrounds, picnic sites and paintball.

FETHIYE

Meğri Lokantası $$ *Eski Cami Gecidi Likya Sok. 8–9, tel: 0252-614 4046.* An old stone house in the market, decorated with kilims and surrounding a central courtyard, this well-established restaurant has a huge choice of Turkish, Asian and international food.

KALKAN

Aubergine $$ *Yacht Liman, Yalıboyu Mah., Kalkan, tel: 0242-844 3332.* A delightful harbour front setting, chic surroundings and an innovative menu have made this one of the best restaurants on the south coast. Open all year.

Ibo Terrace Restaurant $$ *Yalıboyu Mah., Hasan Altan Cad. 32, Kalkan, tel: 0242-844 1343.* Famed not only for its wonderful meze and fish casseroles and its lovely rooftop terrace overlooking Kalkan harbour, but for having the best loos in town.

Gironda $$$ *Yalıboyu Mah., Hasan Altan Cad. 28, tel: 0242-844 1298.* Open 9am–11pm. A beautiful courtyard bar and rooftop terrace with great Ottoman and international food, a good wine cellar, all wrapped up in an old Greek building festooned in bougainvillaea.

KAYA KÖYU

Kaya Wine House $$ *Gökçeburun Mah., 70, Keçiler, tel: 0252-618 0454.* A charming stone house near the famous ghost town that has been restored as a restaurant, with home-cooked dishes prepared according to the produce available each day and a selection of interesting house wines. Advance booking only.

KAŞ

Eriş $$ *Cumhuriyet Meydanı, Uzunçarşı Caddesi, Gürsoy Sokak 13, tel: 0242-836 1057.* A local institution, this friendly traditional restaurant, just behind the harbour at the centre of town, offers a wide range of Turkish casseroles, grills and seafood.

Bahçe $$ *Anıt Mezar Çarşışı, tel: 0242-836 2370* and **Bahçe Balık $$$** *Süleyman Sandiker Sok. 18, Anıt Mezar Çarşışı, tel: 0242-836-2779.* Two excellent related restaurants at the top of the main shopping street, one serving traditional Ottoman food, the other seafood, both with shady garden courtyards. Booking essential.

Güverte Restaurant, Café and Bar $$ *Yaşar Yazıcı Caddesi 4 (Çukurbağ Yanmadasası Yolu Üzeri), tel: 0242-836 3977.* Open all day, this country restaurant has a fabulous location on the Kaş peninsula, with superb sea views, excellent *meze* and seafood.

ÖLÜDENIZ

Buzz Beach Bar and Café *Beachfront, tel: 0252-617 0526.* Frozen margaritas and chocolate cheesecake, a rooftop deck and beachfront restaurant – and live music on Friday and Saturday nights – help make this the place to eat in town.

SAKLIKENT

Kanyon Restaurant $ *opposite canyon entrance, tel: 0252-659 0089.* Open all day, every day, but quiet at night. Simple food (grills and fish) and opportunities for lounging on cushions on rafts beside the river. A wonderful place to idle away the afternoon.

SIDE

Orfoz $$ *Liman Caddesi 581, tel: 0242-753 1362.* Shady harbour front restaurant with wonderful views of the sunset and excellent seafood – no wonder that this favourite has survived while others around it have come and gone.

ULUPINAR

Park Restaurant $$ *Ulupınar (between Kemer and Olympos), tel: 0242-825 7213.* One of a cluster of restaurants near the Olympos turnoff that specialise in trout. Walk down through the pine trees to tables near a stream and watch the fish swim right onto your plate.

INDEX

Berlitz pocket guide

Turkish Coast

First Edition 2009

Written by Melissa Shales
Principal photography by Frank Noon
Series Editor: Tony Halliday

Photography credits
Frank Noon 8, 9, 10, 12, 13, 16, 17, 22, 26, 27, 29, 30, 31, 32, 34, 35, 36, 37, 38, 40, 41, 43, 44, 46, 47, 48–9, 51, 52, 53, 55, 58, 59, 62, 63, 66, 67, 70, 71, 73, 74, 75, 76, 77, 78, 79, 82, 85, 87, 88, 91, 92, 95, 96, 99, 100, 102; iStockPhoto 3MR, 6, 15, 24, 57, 64; akg-images/Cameraphoto 19; Alamy 69; Pete Bennett/Apa 3BR, 60–1, 93; Turkish Culture & Tourism Office 21; Marcus Wilson-Smith 2BR, 3BL, 81

Cover picture: 4Corners Images

Printed in Singapore by Insight Print Services (Pte) Ltd, 38 Joo Koon Road, Singapore 628990. Tel: (65) 6865-1600. Fax: (65) 6861-6438

Berlitz Trademark Reg. U.S. Patent Office and other countries. Marca Registrada

Every effort has been made to provide accurate information in this publication, but changes are inevitable. The publisher cannot be responsible for any resulting loss, inconvenience or injury.

Contact us

At Berlitz we strive to keep our guides as accurate and up to date as possible, but if you find anything that has changed, or if you have any suggestions on ways to improve this guide, then we would be delighted to hear from you.

Berlitz Publishing, PO Box 7910, London SE1 1WE, England.
fax: (44) 20 7403 0290
email: berlitz@apaguide.co.uk
www.berlitzpublishing.com